Accounting Savvy

for Business Owners

Philip B. Goodman CPA

CPA911 Publishing, LLC
Philadelphia PA

Accounting Savvy for Business Owners

ISBN-10: 193292518X

ISBN-13: 978-1932925180

Published by CPA911 Publishing, LLC March 2010

Copyright 2010 CPA911 Publishing, LLC

CPA911 is a Registered Trademark of CPA911 Publishing, LLC.

Table of Contents

Table of Contents

Table of Contents

Table of Contents

Acknowledgments

Cover Design: Matthew Ericson

Production: InfoDesign Services (www.infodesigning.com)

Indexing: After Words Editorial Services (www.aweditorial.com)

Introduction

This book teaches you the bare essentials of accounting principles. It won't teach you enough to pass a CPA exam, and it isn't even designed to provide enough depth of knowledge to get a job as a bookkeeper. It is, in many ways, an oversimplified series of explanations that are only intended to help you understand how accounting principles work.

As a business owner you should understand how transactions should be created, how records should be kept, and how to interpret the totals you see when you look at financial reports. Without this knowledge, it's difficult to track and understand your business finances.

The topics covered represent the questions that are most often asked of accountants by their clients. Thousands of business owners write to www.cpa911.com (part of CPA911 Publishing, LLC) to ask how to resolve problems, understand reports, and create transactions accurately. Thousands of accountants write also; to ask how to explain bookkeeping tasks to their confused clients, and also to ask how to straighten out books that are totally inaccurate because business owners have entered transactions incorrectly. Therefore, this book could accurately be called an FAQ of the ABCs of accounting.

Being able to rely on accurate financial records is absolutely crucial to the success of any business. Accounting figures aren't just for preparing tax returns. You need to keep an eye on the amount of money owed to you by your customers, you must be able to see where your highest profits are made, and you must be able to determine where your expenses may be inappropriately high (or perhaps too low; you may not be spending enough to grow or to manage growth).

Lastly, if you don't understand accounting principles, and you don't know how to "read" your books, you're a potential victim of anyone who wants to cheat you. Sadly, this happens more often in small businesses than most people realize, even in businesses that employ family members to manage the finances.

Dedication

Thank you to Kathy Ivens for approaching me to write this book and her work on its content. It would not have been possible without her patience and guidance through this entire process, my initial effort at publication.

My love for accounting comes from relationships established over 30 years working closely with family owned businesses and nonprofit organizations whose desire to understand their budgeting process and financial statements have taught me to get beyond the accounting jargon and explain things in ways they can understand. I am eternally grateful for the confidence they have placed in me and all they have taught me.

Lastly, a special thanks to my wife, Pennye, whose encouragement and support has allowed me to pursue my profession in a way that frequently has kept me away from her and our family.

Philip B. Goodman CPA

Chapter 1

Basic Accounting Rules

Business accounting is based on a double entry system of bookkeeping. This means that for every entry you make there must be an equal and opposite entry. Opposite refers to the other side of the ledger.

The Ledger

The ledger sides are labeled DEBIT (always on the left) and CREDIT (always on the right), and you must make sure that every transaction has equal entries posted to both sides of the ledger.

If you do your bookkeeping manually, or in a spreadsheet program, you must enter both sides of the ledger. If you use checkwriting software (such as Quicken) you should move those transactions into a manual system or a spreadsheet program in order to enter transactions to both sides of the ledger accurately (or, even better, invest in real accounting software).

If you use accounting software, you usually have to enter only one side of the transaction because your setup and configuration of the software pre-determines the postings. For most transactions the software takes care of the "other side" of the entry for you automatically, so you don't even have to think about it. (The exception is a journal entry which is generally used to adjust existing figures in the ledger.) However, you *do* have to assign the appropriate account to a transaction, which means you have to understand the way accounting transactions work in order to set up your software properly.

Every transaction falls into a category that has a default or "natural" side of the ledger, as seen in Table 1-1. These categories are explained in this chapter.

DEBIT	CREDIT
ASSETS	
	LIABILITIES
	EQUITY
	INCOME
EXPENSES	

Table 1-1: Each category has a "natural" side of the ledger.

The information in Table 1-1 is the basis for all accounting whether your business is a multi-national corporation or an ice cream stand on the beach. All accounting processes follow the rules inherent in this chart, although large companies have many subcategories to refine and narrow the postings made in their accounting system.

When a category *increases* as a result of a transaction, the amount is posted to its assigned (default) side of the ledger; when it *decreases* as a result of a transaction, the amount is posted to the opposite side of the ledger.

For example, when you enter a transaction that adds an amount to your bank account, the increase in your bank balance is posted to the Debit side of the ledger (because your bank account is an asset and the Debit side is the default side for assets).

The offsetting entry is the "reason" for the transaction, which in this case is usually the receipt of business income (notice that income is on the Credit side of the ledger, and because income is increased, it is posted to its default side of the ledger).

On the other hand, when you remove money from your bank, that transaction decreases the value of that asset, so the amount is posted to the "other" (in this case, Credit) side of the ledger. The equal and opposite entry is the "reason" for the decrease, such as payment of an expense (notice that expenses are on the Debit side of the ledger, and since expenses have been increased by the transaction, you use the default side for that category).

Making Sense of the Debit and Credit Labels

The labels *Debit* and *Credit* can be confusing because they don't follow the logic of your generally accepted definitions for those words. How can an asset be a debit, isn't *debit* a negative word?

These terms are used all over the world, and date back to the 1400's; so it's too late to try to change them. Just live with them. The solution is to ignore your vocabulary skills (and your logic) and just memorize the rules and definitions. You'll be amazed at how fast you absorb the concepts once you've begun entering, or examining, business transactions. There are only two rules you have to memorize:

- Debits on the left, Credits on the right.

- Assets and expenses are debits by default; liabilities, equity, and income are credits by default.

Accounting Categories

Every transaction posts to both sides of the ledger, using at least one category on each side. Some of the category labels are rather broad, so in this section I'll define them more specifically.

Assets

Assets are things that belong to (are owned by) your business, and they are broken down into two main subcategories called Current Assets and Long Term Assets. In turn, each of those subcategories has additional subcategories. Chapter 5 teaches you when and how to use asset accounts in transactions.

Current Assets

Current assets are best described as those things that you expect to be able to convert to cash, or use as cash, within one year. These are the assets that are commonly used when you're posting transactions. The following are examples of common current assets:

- Cash, which includes money in bank accounts, in the cash register, and in the petty cash box.

- Accounts Receivable, which is the money currently owed to you by customers.

- Inventory, which is the total value of the cost of products you purchased for resale or you purchased to create a product.

- Loans you make to others.

- Prepaid expenses, which are the monies you paid in advance of their actual use such as prepayments on insurance premiums, payment of business tax estimates for the current year's taxes, deposits on utility accounts, and other similar prepayments.

Long Term Assets

Long term assets are those possessions that you expect to remain in use, without converting them to cash, for more than a year. The following are common examples of long term assets:

- Land

- Buildings (and accumulated depreciation)

- Leasehold Improvements (and accumulated depreciation)

- Equipment (and accumulated depreciation)

- Vehicles (and accumulated depreciation)

- Furniture and Fixtures (and accumulated depreciation)

- Start Up Costs (and accumulated amortization)

- Goodwill (and accumulated amortization)

- Copyrights and Patents (and accumulated amortization)

You learn about tracking assets in Chapter 5, and Chapter 10 explains depreciation and amortization.

Liabilities

A liability is something that you may be holding, or have the use of, but does not belong to you. It is something you owe to someone else. Like assets, liabilities are subcategorized into two groups: Current Liabilities and Long Term Liabilities. Chapter 6 discusses the whens, hows, and whys of posting transactions to liability accounts.

Current Liabilities

Current liabilities are usually defined as debts due within a year. Following are the common current liabilities you track:

- Accounts Payable, which is money you owe vendors.

- Payroll Liabilities, which is money withheld from employees' pay, your business' share of taxes on that pay, and other payroll obligations due to government agencies, insurance companies, pension funds, etc.

- Sales tax you have collected from customers and must turn over to the state tax authority.

Long Term Liabilities

Long term liabilities are debts that require more than a year to pay off. These are commonly loans such as mortgages, business loans, lines of credit, equipment loans, vehicle loans, etc.

Equity

Equity tracks the value of business ownership and the value of the business. The way you track equity, including the types of categories and ledger accounts you create, depends on the way your business is organized. Following are some of the common equity categories:

- Stock in your company, if you are a corporation.

- Capital invested by partners if you are a partnership, limited liability partnership (LLP), or limited liability company (LLC).

- Capital invested by you if you are a proprietorship or single-member LLC.

- Draws (withdrawals of funds) if you are not incorporated.

- Retained earnings, which is the accumulated profit (or loss) since the business began. This is a calculated amount (income less expenses), not an account to which you normally post transactions.

Chapter 7 explains the various types of business organizations and explains when and how to post transactions to equity accounts.

Income

Income is the revenue your business receives. You can separate your income into various subcategories in order to analyze the source of funds. For example, if you sell both products and services, you may want to track those monies separately. If you sell services only, you may want to subcategorize your revenue by service type.

In addition to the subcategories you set up to track specific revenue sources, it's common to create an Other Income subcategory to cover uncommon "miscellaneous" income receipts that aren't connected to your main source of revenue. For example, you may want to create a category for Interest Income or Finance Charges Collected.

In addition, you may want to track customer returns and refunds as its own category, instead of posting the amounts of those returns to the regular Income category (which produces a running total of the net sales). Chapter 3 discusses the ways to post income transactions.

Expenses

Expenses are the monies you spend to run your business. Expenses are subcategorized for the purposes of meeting the reporting requirements on tax returns and for your own analysis.

Generally we think of expenses in two main categories - Cost of Goods Sold and General and Administrative Expenses.

Cost of Goods Sold

Sometimes called Cost of Sales, this is an expense category that usually tracks what you spend to create a product that you sell from inventory. Commonly, the following expenses are tracked as Cost of Goods Sold:

- Cost of raw materials for manufacturing.

- Cost of goods you purchase for resale.

- Inbound shipping costs for raw materials or products for resale to your business.

- Cost of labor to manufacture and assemble materials into products.

- Other costs involved with creating an inventory item, such as packaging, crating, etc.

Sometimes businesses can track Cost of Goods even if they're not selling inventory items. Check with your accountant about the Cost of Goods subcategories that are appropriate for your business.

General and Administrative Expenses

The general expenses involved in running your business are tracked by category in order to calculate totals that are required for tax returns, and also to track specific types of expenses so you can analyze the way you're spending money to run your business. Some of the commonly used categories are the following:

- Advertising
- Bank service charges
- Dues and subscriptions
- Entertainment (of customers, not your own fun)
- Insurance
- Interest expense
- Legal and accounting services
- Office Supplies
- Employer payroll taxes
- Postage and shipping
- Rent
- Subcontractors
- Telephone
- Travel
- Vehicle maintenance
- Web site expenses

You and your accountant can design the list of expenses you need to track your expenses intelligently, and to prepare tax returns easily.

In addition, it's common to have an expense category called Other Expenses, in which you track subcategories less commonly used in transactions. For example, you may want to track monies expended in the following subcategories as Other Expenses instead of putting these expenses in the general expense category list:

- Business Taxes
- Fines and Penalties

For most businesses, the list of expense categories is quite long (and the more detail-oriented you want to be as you track and analyze where you spend money, the longer it gets). Some individual transactions cover multiple expense categories (think about entering the transaction that occurs when you write a check to your credit card company). Chapter 4 covers the ways in which you use these expense categories when you're entering transactions.

Cash Basis Vs. Accrual Basis Accounting

An accounting method is a set of rules used to determine when income and expenses are reported to the IRS. You can use either cash basis or accrual basis as your accounting method.

You don't really get to decide on an accounting method, because you can't flip a coin, nor can you decide based on what seems easier or more advantageous to your tax bill. There are rules about the accounting method you use and those rules are created and enforced by the IRS. If you do your own tax returns, you should consult an accountant before determining which accounting method to use.

You declare your accounting method when you file your first tax return for your business. If you want to change your accounting method after that you must apply to the IRS for permission to do so. The IRS provides forms for this purpose. (Sometimes, albeit rarely, the IRS contacts businesses and orders them to change their accounting method.)

You must use the same accounting method across the board, which means you can't opt to use the cash basis method for income and the accrual method for expenses (or the other way around).

In this section, I'll explain the differences between these two accounting methods, and then go over the guidelines for the types of businesses that must choose a specific accounting method.

NOTE: If you're using, or planning to use, accounting software, some software lets you switch between cash and accrual basis reports. This means you can see the state of your business finances by creating accrual reports, and then create cash basis reports for filing your taxes (which is the prevalent tax accounting basis for a small business). QuickBooks, the most popular software for small business, is one of the accounting software applications that provide an accounting method choice for many financial reports.

Cash Basis Accounting

The cash basis accounting method is used by most small businesses. Cash basis accounting means you account for income when you receive it and you account for expenses when you pay them.

In cash basis accounting your income for the tax year includes all revenue you receive during that year, regardless of when you sold services or products and sent an invoice to the customer. It's the date on which you receive the money that determines the year in which you report it. The date on which you deposit the money doesn't count because you're not allowed to avoid increasing your revenue (and therefore not paying tax on it) by holding onto checks, cash, credit card sales slips, etc.

and depositing them in the next year. The operative word for declaring revenue is "received", the customer's invoice date and the deposit date don't count.

For example, if you have a sale to a customer in November or December and create an invoice at that time, the amount of the invoice is not considered income if you use cash basis accounting. Instead, you recognize the income when you receive your customer's payment, which may not be until sometime in the next year.

If you collect sales tax your state's sales tax law determines when that sales tax is recorded. The state doesn't care which accounting method you use for reporting business income. Some states consider sales tax due when it's invoiced (accrual based accounting), and other states consider sales tax due when you receive payment from the customer (cash based accounting). Check the terms on your state sales tax license to learn how you should be tracking and remitting sales tax (and read Chapter 3 to learn how to enter those transactions).

Your business expenses are deducted in the year you pay them. It doesn't matter when the vendor sent a bill, you deduct the expense in the year you write the check (the date on your check is what counts) or hand over cash (don't forget to get a dated receipt when you use cash).

Accrual Basis Accounting

Accrual basis accounting is a more precise way of keeping books than cash basis accounting, because it takes into consideration every transaction and event as it occurs. When you view your records, or create reports, you see all the transactions you've created and posted, which makes it easier to analyze the health of your business.

In accrual basis accounting, your income is recorded when you earn it, either by performing a service or selling a product. When you create an invoice for a customer, you've earned the income and you report it in the year you earned it, even if the customer doesn't pay you until next year.

Your expenses are recorded when you become liable for them, regardless of when you actually pay them. When you receive a bill from a vendor, you're liable for the expense and you report the expense for the year in which you received the bill, based on the date of the bill, even if you don't pay the bill until the following year. The same is true for expenses for which you don't receive an invoice but you know your date of liability, such as rent, interest payments on a loan, etc.

Selecting an Accounting Method

Determining the accounting method is a matter of matching your business operations with the IRS rules. Some of the rules are clear; others may seem a bit confusing and hard to interpret. Most small businesses use cash basis accounting, but if you can't determine for sure which accounting method to use, consult an accountant.

Following is a very brief (and very oversimplified) summary of the scenarios in which the IRS insists on accrual basis accounting for calculating your tax liability. In actuality the rules are more complicated than set out here, and include exceptions for certain business types. You must get professional advice for this decision. If your business clearly doesn't fit into one of these descriptions, you can almost certainly keep books and file taxes using the cash basis accounting method.

- Any corporation (other than an S corporation) that has average annual gross receipts exceeding

$5 million must use the accrual basis accounting method.

- Any partnership that includes a corporation as a partner (other than an S corporation), that has average annual gross receipts exceeding $5 million must use the accrual basis accounting method.

- Most businesses that sell products tracked in inventory must use accrual basis accounting for transactions that involve inventory. Some inventory-based businesses must use accrual basis accounting entirely; other inventory-based businesses are permitted to use cash basis accounting for non-inventory transactions. Check with an accountant to determine which of these scenarios applies to your inventory-based business. (Chapter 8 discusses the way you track inventory purchases, materials, and sales.)

NOTE: The IRS has a chart to compute "average annual gross receipts".

Fiscal Vs. Calendar Year

You don't have to use the calendar year as the basis of your bookkeeping reports and your tax filing. Instead, you may be able to use a fiscal year, determining the first month of the year for yourself. If you run your business on a fiscal year, you create year end reports and file your taxes based on your fiscal calendar.

While it's not common for a small business to use a fiscal year instead of the calendar year (either because of habit or

IRS rules), there may be circumstances in which this option is preferable.

WARNING: If you opt to run your business on a fiscal year, you must still keep payroll records and file payroll forms on a calendar year basis. The same rule applies to subcontractors you pay who receive Form 1099. All accounting software is able to handle this scenario.

Most businesses that adopt a fiscal year do so because of their annual business cycle or in order to avoid facing year end tasks and tax preparation chores during their busiest times of the year. This almost exclusively applies to retailers who have a surge of sales activity in November and December (and perhaps even part of January), and aren't prepared to devote the personnel and time needed to perform the intensive work involved in using a December 31 year end date for closing the books and preparing reports for taxes.

Nonprofit organizations and government agencies almost always use a fiscal year that coincides with periods of activity and spending. School districts often adopt a fiscal year that begins July 1 and ends June 30. Governments use fiscal years also; for example the U.S. government's fiscal year begins October 1 and ends September 30.

NOTE: If you use a fiscal year you note that fact in reports by using the term FYxxxx, where xxxx is the year in which your fiscal year ends.

Chapter 2

Accounting Components

• •

An accounting system is the structure of records that create the financial information for a business. Accounting functions are bottom-up tasks that start on the lowest level (entering individual transactions), and feed the information up through higher-level structures (journals and ledgers). Figure 2-1 shows a simple representation of the "from the bottom up" flow of information, and I explain these components in this chapter.

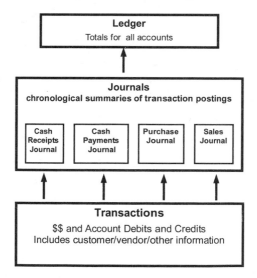

Figure 2-1: The data in a transaction flows through the components of your accounting system.

Chart of Accounts

The chart of accounts is the list of account names you use to keep your accounting records. Each name in the list represents a category for the type of transactions that are collected for that name. For example, there are accounts for assets (bank account, equipment), liabilities (loans payable, sales tax payable), income (sales), and expenses (payroll, rent, etc.).

Although the chart of accounts is merely a list of names (and numbers, if you elect to use a numbered chart of accounts), it is the foundation of your ledger (usually called the *General Ledger*). All of your individual transaction postings make up the totals in your general ledger.

Linking a transaction to an account is called *posting*. For instance, when you deposit money from the sale of goods or services into your bank, you post the transaction amount to the bank that's in your chart of accounts (that's the debit side of the transaction), and the income category in your chart of accounts (that's the credit side). When you send a check to the landlord, you post the transaction to the expense named Rent (the debit side) in your chart of accounts, and remove the money from the bank (the credit side).

Naming Accounts

When you name your accounts, create names that are descriptive and easy to understand. This makes it easier to post transactions and also makes it easier to understand reports.

Use names that clearly describe the types of postings you'll make to the account. For example, an account named Telephone is a better choice than Communications Expenses. Computer Expenses is too generic for an account name if you want to analyze where your dollars are going; instead, create separate accounts for computer repairs & parts, computer support plans, computer software, and so on.

Be especially careful about clarity when you name your asset and liability accounts. For example, if you have a loan, name the account so it's easy to determine which loan it represents. I've seen businesses name a liability account Bank Loan for a loan or line of credit and then when they have another type of loan from the same bank (perhaps for a vehicle) they call it Bank Loan 2. This makes it difficult for the person entering the transaction to know how to post it; unfortunately, rather than investigate, many users just guess.

I suggest you include either the last four digits of the loan's account number (Loan Payable XYZ Bank-1234) or the monthly payment amount (Loan Payable XYZ Bank-123/mo) in your account name. The same clarity should apply to naming assets. Don't name an asset Money Due to Company; instead describe the purpose of the asset account, such as Deposits Held by Vendors.

Using Account Numbers

Many accountants, and some accounting software applications, insist on creating a chart of accounts that has numbers attached to the account names. Using numbers means you can control the way the account names are sorted (because sorting alphabetically doesn't let you put related accounts together).

For example, if accounts of the type Expense are arranged numerically instead of alphabetically, you can list related expense accounts contiguously. All of your insurance categories are together, as are your employer payroll expenses, your general office expenses, and so on. When you use account numbers to make these related categories contiguous, you can generate subtotals that make it easier to analyze your cost of doing business by broad general categories. If your related categories are numbered in a way that you can create subtotals that match the categories required on your company's tax return, this is also useful (especially to your accountant, who will spend less time on your tax return, which saves you money!).

Creating a Numbering Scheme

The numbers you assign to accounts give you a quick clue about the type and category of the account you're working with. As you create accounts, you must use the numbers intelligently, assigning ranges of numbers to account types. The most common approach to account numbering uses the following pattern:

- 1xxx Assets
- 2xxx Liabilities
- 3xxx Equity
- 4xxx Income
- 5xxx Expenses (can be of a specific type)
- 6xxx Expenses (can be of a specific type)
- 7xxx Expenses (can be of a specific type)
- 8xxx Expenses (can be of a specific type)
- 9xxx Other Income and Expenses (a way to track 'miscellaneous' income and expenses such as late fees, penalties, rebates, etc.)

You can, if you wish, have a variety of expense types and reserve the starting number for specific types. For example, some companies use 5*xxx* for sales expenses (they even separate the payroll postings between the sales people and the rest of the employees), then use 6000 through 7999 for general operating expenses, and 8*xxx* for other specific expenses that are inter-related (such as business taxes).

Some companies that track inventory use 5xxx for Cost of Goods Sold and begin grouping general expenses with 6xxx.

You need to design an easy to understand format to break down assets. You might use 1000 through 1099 for cash accounts, 1100 through 1699 for receivables and other current assets, then use 1700 through 1799 for tracking fixed assets such as equipment, furniture, and so on.

Follow the same pattern for liabilities, starting with current liabilities and moving to long term. It's also a good idea to keep all the payroll withholding liabilities together with a set of contiguous numbers.

TIP: As you create accounts, increase the previous account number by 10, so that if your first bank account is 1000, the next bank account is 1010, and so on. These intervals give you room to create additional accounts that belong in the same general area of your chart of accounts. If you have a great many accounts, use more than four digits in your account numbers.

Divisionalized Chart of Accounts

If you use account numbers, you can create divisions within your chart of accounts. This means the account numbers can be linked to divisions or departments of your business that you want to track separately.

For example, you may have offices or stores in multiple locations and you want to know the financial totals (sales and expenses) for each location. Some businesses want to track financial information separately for wholesale and retail customers. Contractors often want to track business profits between repairs and construction. Other businesses have other types of divisions or departments and they want to see the profits (or loss) for each type.

TIP: Almost all accounting software applications provide a way to divide the chart of accounts into divisions. The exception is QuickBooks, which offers a feature called Class Tracking (calling each division a "class") but it is very limited and doesn't produce reports for assets, liabilities, or equity accounts on a class-by-class basis.

Chart of Accounts Divisional Mask

You have to design a divisionalized chart of accounts by creating a *mask*, which is the format of the account numbers. For example, you may design a mask in the following format:

XXXX-YY, where XXXX is the account number and YY is the number you've assigned to the division. If you use five digits for your account numbers, the mask would be XXXXX-YY. If you have more than 100 divisions, you could use the mask XXXX-YYY.

If you have multiple locations and you're also tracking departments for each location (e.g. Wholesale/Retail or any other subset of activity you want to track), you can create a mask that has three sections:

XXXX-YY-ZZ

NOTE: Some accounting software programs limit the number of sections available for the mask, and almost all accounting programs limit the number of characters available for account numbers (which has an effect on the number of characters available in each section of the mask).

Creating the Chart of Account Divisions

You need to assign a number to each division, and the number of characters must equal the number of characters you decided on for the divisional mask. You accomplish this by using leading zeroes instead of using a single digit. For example, if your division mask has two characters, your division numbers are 01, 02, etc.; for a three character division mask, use 001, 002, etc.

You need a company-wide account for each account, and that company-wide account is where the totals for all divisions are maintained). This account has the divisional number 00 (or 000 if your divisional mask is three characters).

For example, if you have two locations, you might have the following accounts for rent expense:

- 6100 Rent – 00
- 6100 Rent – 01
- 6100 Rent – 02

Many accounting software applications that support a divisionalized chart of accounts have a setup routine that makes it easier to build your chart of accounts properly. The setup routine usually covers the following steps:

- It walks you through the process of creating the mask (the number of sections and the number of characters for each section).

- It asks for the name of each division, and the number you want to assign to that division.

- It automatically creates all the divisional accounts for every account already entered in your chart of accounts (assigning 00 to the original account to make it the company-wide account).

- It automatically creates all the divisional accounts for new accounts you create.

If your accounting application doesn't have a setup routine, or if you don't have accounting software and you're building your chart of accounts manually (including Excel), use these explanations as your guidelines.

Posting to a Divisionalized Chart of Accounts

Posting transactions to a divisionalized chart of accounts requires a bit more care than posting to a standard chart of accounts. However, the payback is the ability to create extremely useful reports that can help you analyze your business.

Some transactions are easy to post, such as sales transactions that came from a specific division, or disbursements to a vendor for services or products that are for a specific division. For example, if you're tracking multiple locations, the utilities and rent are probably linked to a specific location.

Some of the transactions you create won't post neatly into a single divisional account. This is especially true of disbursements (you can almost always post income directly to the division that generated the income).

Often, you post transactions to the company-wide account because you don't care about the specific division for that transaction (transactions involving asset, liability, or equity accounts commonly post to the company-wide accounts). Sometimes, you post to the company-wide account because you'll allocate the total amount of the transaction across divisions at the end of the period (year, quarter, or month).

Chapter 10, which covers year-end journal entries, explains how to allocate expenses across divisions.

Transactions

A transaction is any event that takes place that involves your company's financial state. All transactions have a "source document" such as a check to a vendor, an invoice to a customer, or a cash sale transaction for a customer (no invoice because payment is made at the time of the sale).

All transactions have to be "balanced", which means that whatever amount you're dealing with has two sides: a debit side and a credit side. The total amount of one side must equal the total amount of the other side. Of course, that means that a minimum of two accounts in your general ledger are involved in every transaction.

A financial transaction can be a sale of goods or services, paying an expense to a vendor, a transfer of money from one bank account to another, remitting money you're holding to a government agency (e.g. payroll taxes or sales tax), or any of numerous other things that occur as you conduct business. Specific instructions for creating and managing all these types of transactions are found throughout this book.

If you use accounting software, when you enter simple transactions (such as invoices, customer payments, or vendor payments) you usually have to enter only one side of the transaction; the software is already configured to enter the other side for you.

If you don't use accounting software, you have to enter both sides of the transaction. This is true whether you're keeping your books in a spreadsheet program such as Excel, or you're keeping your books on paper.

NOTE: Check writing programs such as Quicken don't post to both sides of a general ledger, and don't really provide a way for you to accomplish this task and produce a general ledger report. Even though they can provide some category totals, these applications are designed for personal use and personal tax returns, not for business use or business tax returns.

Journals

Journals are reports on the amounts posted to categories (accounts) by individual transactions. The journal is where the transaction enters the accounting system and it contains the information needed to move totals to the general ledger. (Journals are sometimes referred to as *the books of original entry*.) Journals are kept in chronological order.

Types of Journals

Back in the old days, before accounting software was available for small businesses at a reasonable price, accounting tasks were done manually in books designed for that purpose (every page had columns). At minimum, the following journals usually existed:

- **Cash Receipts Journal** for posting money received, such as cash sales, and payments of customer invoices. In addition, refunds and rebates from vendors are usually posted as cash receipts.

- **Cash Payments Journal** for posting money disbursed, such as cash from the cash register, checks that are paying vendor bills that were

entered into the system, or checks that are direct
disbursements (no vendor bill exists in the
system).

• **Sales Journal** for posting customer invoices.

• **Purchases Journal** for posting vendor bills.

Today, there are still many small business owners who
do bookkeeping "semi-manually", which means that they use
computers, but they don't use a business accounting software
program. They use Excel, or a check-writing program such as
Quicken.

If you use Excel, your accounting tasks will be easier
if you duplicate the journals within an Excel spreadsheet by
creating separate worksheets. If you're using a check-writing
program, you should also use Excel to create journals so you
can categorize your transactions, with subtotals, to match the
way you want to analyze your business and to track totals for tax
returns.

Journal Entries From Transactions

Every transaction you enter results in a journal entry. For
example, if you created a check to pay the rent, the journal for
the transaction resembles the journal in Table 2-1.

Account	Debit	Credit
1000 – Bank Account		800.00
6000 – Rent	800.00	

Table 2-1: The journal tracks each transaction you
create.

If you use accounting software, the journal is created automatically. In fact, in addition to tracking the accounts involved in each transaction, accounting software can provide reports about transactions for other entities in your bookkeeping records, such as the customer, vendor, inventory item, and so on.

> **TIP**: Many accounting software applications let you view the journal from the original transaction's window. For example, in QuickBooks you can open a transaction and press Ctrl-Y to see the journal.

Journals can track additional information you record in addition to the accounts and amounts, such as the reference number for the source document (invoice number, check number) and the vendor or customer involved in the transaction.

Direct Journal Entries

It's also possible to create a journal entry (often called a *JE or AJE* for Adjusting Journal Entry) to post amounts to the general ledger. Journal entries are used to adjust existing numbers; they're not normally used in the course of your daily business to record individual transactions.

> **NOTE**: It's best to let your accountant enter JEs (or provide specific instructions for you to follow).

For example, when you depreciate or amortize an asset, no "real" transaction takes place; there's no check written, no money moves in or out of your bank account, and no customer or vendor is involved. Table 2-2 is an example of a depreciation JE.

Account	Debit	Credit
Accum Dep - Furn & Fixtures		1800.00
Accum Dep - Vehicles		1500.00
Accum Dep - Equipment		2000.00
Depreciation Expense	5300.00	

Table 2-2: You need to use a journal entry to enter depreciation.

Chapter 10 covers the common year-end journal entries that businesses create.

General Ledger

The general ledger is the final location of financial data. It collects all the financial data from the journals and contains the total of all transactions posted to each account in the chart of accounts.

You *prove* (check the accuracy of) the general ledger by creating a *trial balance*, which should show the total amount of debits equal to the total amount of credits. Figure 2-2 is an example of a trial balance.

More information on creating the trial balance and other important financial reports from the general ledger is in Chapter 11.

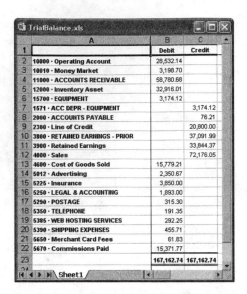

TrialBalance.xls		
A	B	C
	Debit	Credit
10000 · Operating Account	28,532.14	
10010 · Money Market	3,198.70	
11000 · ACCOUNTS RECEIVABLE	58,780.68	
12000 · Inventory Asset	32,916.01	
15700 · EQUIPMENT	3,174.12	
1571 · ACC DEPR - EQUIPMENT		3,174.12
2000 · ACCOUNTS PAYABLE		76.21
2300 · Line of Credit		20,800.00
3800 · RETAINED EARNINGS - PRIOR		37,091.99
3900 · Retained Earnings		33,844.37
4000 · Sales		72,176.05
4600 · Cost of Goods Sold	15,779.21	
5012 · Advertising	2,350.67	
5225 · Insurance	3,850.00	
5250 · LEGAL & ACCOUNTING	1,893.00	
5290 · POSTAGE	315.30	
5350 · TELEPHONE	191.35	
5385 · WEB HOSTING SERVICES	292.25	
5390 · SHIPPING EXPENSES	455.71	
5650 · Merchant Card Fees	61.83	
5670 · Commissions Paid	15,371.77	
	167,162.74	167,162.74

Figure 2-2: In a trial balance, the total debits must equal the total credits.

Chapter 3

Tracking Income

• •

Your business gets its income from customers, and most businesses need to track the activity of each customer in addition to tracking income dollars. In this chapter I'll discuss setting up customer records properly, and I'll explain the accounting processes that take place when you receive income.

Creating Customers

Unless you're running a retail operation, and never send invoices (instead you collect your money at the time of the sale), you have to keep track of customer activity. You need to know which customers are required to pay sales tax, the sales tax rate for each customer, and which customers have unpaid invoices.

In some businesses, customer prices differ (your retail customers might have a different price level from wholesale customers), so you should track the price level for each customer. You need to track money you owe customers due to credits you issued for returned goods. Some customers have shipping addresses that differ from their billing addresses. Whew! All this information (and even more information, depending on your type of business) should be included in each customer's record.

Naming Customers

Every customer in your system must have a unique name. If you're using accounting software, the customer setup screen has a field for the customer name, and then other fields for other information related to that customer name (company name, address, phone, etc.).

Because each customer has to be unique, think of the customer name as the customer "code" (many accounting software programs actually use the word "code" in the "name this customer" field so there's absolutely no confusion about the way to use the field). Other fields in the customer record provide the customer's name, address, and so on.

Some businesses have a difficult time coming up with unique customer codes because so many of their customers have similar (or even identical) names. If you sell supplies to pizza stores, many of your customers might have company names that start with Pizza.

One way to insure uniqueness is to use another reference that is unique; the most common solution is to use the telephone number (including the area code) in the customer code.

Required Customer Data

You must track all customer data that is related to customer transactions; in addition, you can maintain customer data that you can use for marketing and advertising.

Name and Address

If you send invoices you must maintain information about the customer's company name (or full name if the customer is an individual), billing address, and shipping address. If you take credit cards on an Internet shopping cart or over the telephone you will also need the name and billing address associated with your customer's credit card, which could be different from the business name and address (you don't need this information for over-the-counter credit card sales because you have the credit card).

Terms

You must specify the terms of payment, either the number of days available for payment from the date of the invoice, or a specific day of the following month by which payment is due. If you provide discounts for early payment, note the amount of the discount and the time period for which the discount is valid.

Sales Tax Status

Some customers are taxable and other customers are not, and each customer's record must contain the tax status. The obvious "not taxable" list includes the following:

- Nonprofit organizations.

- Government agencies.

- Out of state customers whose addresses are not in a state that has a reciprocal agreement for sales tax with your state.

- Customers who resell the products they buy from you and who have provided their sales tax license numbers to you. (That sales tax license number must be part of the customer's record.)

Remember that a customer deemed "taxable" doesn't always owe tax on a sales transaction. The goods or services you're selling a taxable customer must also have a status of "taxable" for sales tax to be added to the sales transaction. Some states tax almost everything, including services. Some states eliminate some goods from taxation (usually necessities), and other states eliminate many services from taxation.

Sales Tax Rate

You have to note the sales tax rates for each customer. Depending on where you do business, the effort involved in determining a customer's sales tax rate ranges from mildly confusing to totally baffling.

You need to make sure you understand your state's sales tax rules. Most states have adopted a series of confusing and convoluted rules about the tax rate applied to taxable transactions. You must also be aware of the rules in your customers' states, and those states' definitions of whether you have a business presence in those states. Depending on the circumstances, you may be liable for charging, collecting, and remitting sales taxes to the customers' home state.

Many states have a base tax rate, and then impose an additional tax you must add to the base rate (and the total of the two rates is applied to sales of taxable goods and services). This surtax is based on location. In some states, certain counties or cities impose an additional tax (usually at a different rate), while other counties and cities don't. Some states use smaller locations, such as zip codes. In many states, the surtax is not the same for each location within the state.

A few states base the tax rate location on the vendor's location (that's you). Whatever the tax rate is for your location is the rate you use to apply sales tax to your customer transactions. If your location rate is not the same as the rate for the location of your customer (whose business may be in the next county), you still have to charge the customer your rate. If this is the rule in your state, then setting up your customers' tax rate is an easy task.

Some states base the tax rate on the location of the customer's billing address (or main business address). This too, is easy to determine and enter into the customer's record as the customer's tax rate.

Some states base the tax rate on the location of the delivery of goods or services. If your customer has a shipping address that's different from the billing address, and the shipping address location has a different tax rate, enter the tax rate for the shipping address in the customer's record. But wait, suppose the customer has multiple shipping addresses, each in a different location, and each location has a different sales tax rate? There's no easy solution for this; in the end, you need to keep notes on the multiple shipping address tax rates and use the appropriate address as the customer's tax rate.

After you've determined the combination of state tax and local surtax for this customer, you can record the customer's tax rate in the customer's record. Then, things get muddy.

Remember that in order to add sales tax to a transaction, both the customer and the goods or services you're selling must be taxable. Even when you know the sale is taxable and you know the customer's tax rate, the confusion continues.

Some states have different tax rates for different types of goods or services; this means each item on a sales transaction could have a unique tax rate. You have to calculate and apply the sales tax on a line-by-line basis instead of calculating the tax on the total sale. If you're using accounting software, the system automatically calculates tax on the total sale and won't let you remove it; in that case you must create a sales tax item of zero percent and apply it to this transaction.

When you change the tax rate for a transaction, some accounting software displays a message asking whether you want to apply the tax rate to the customer. Click No unless this customer's purchases are always for specific items that have their own unique tax rates. If you're in a business where specific tax rates are always applied in your state (such as a hotel or a bar), it's usually fine to assign a zero tax rate to all your customers, especially if you track your sales in a batch, using a generic customer name. Do *not* configure the customer as non-taxable, because the taxable items won't generate a sales tax. Instead, apply the zero percent tax to a taxable customer. (Remember: In order to apply sales tax, both the customer and the item must be taxable.)

Some states tax only the first XX dollars of a product, and then either reduce the tax or eliminate it. For example, only the first $5000.00 of the sale of tangible property may be taxable. However, if the state sales tax has a limit, the local surtax may not recognize that limit. Or, some local surtaxes may recognize the limit, others may not, and some may have a different limit.

Additional complications arise when you have to remit the sales tax to the state. Some states require you to send separate payments to each tax location. Most states want totals that show both the state's base tax rate and the location surtaxes, along with the total of nontaxable sales and taxable sales for each location. Most accounting software handles this smoothly, but if you're not using accounting software (or you don't understand the way your software is reporting sales tax liability) instructions for remitting sales tax are in Chapter 6.

TIP: There are companies that provide software that can calculate the sales tax due on each sales transaction automatically. Use your favorite Internet search engine to look for "sales tax software".

Optional Customer Data

If you're using accounting software, the more information you've configured in a customer record, the easier it is to create transactions. Most software automatically prefills data in transaction forms for certain types of data, such as the credit limit, the preferred shipping method, the preferred payment method, and so on.

WARNING: Don't keep customer credit card information in the customer record unless you're using accounting software that automatically hides all but the last four digits of the card number. Users with the right permissions and the right password can view the full number.

Most accounting software programs let you specify whether the customer should be sent monthly statements. This configuration option makes statements automatic because you don't have to select or deselect customers every time you create statements.

Many accounting software programs let you specify whether the customer accepts backorders, and if so, how to handle backorders. The usual options are the following:

- Hold the order until the backorder can be filled

- Ship what's available and send backordered products separately

- No backorders, just ship what's available and ignore the rest of the order

This makes it easier and faster to ship and invoice goods when you don't have sufficient quantity to deliver the entire order. If you have customers with a "no backorders" option, be sure to send a note or call them when the product is available; usually that results in a new order.

Almost all accounting software lets you specify a customer "type", which you can use anyway you please. For example, you might use customer types Wholesale and Retail, or separate customer types by the type of services you perform for them. You can produce reports by customer type, or send correspondence about special sales or other information to specific customer types.

Invoice Journals

An invoice is a document showing the details of goods and services purchased by the customer and it includes a reference number (the invoice number), the goods and services sold, quantities, prices, taxes, total amount due, the transaction date, and the terms of sale.

In most cases, invoices are sent to customers after the goods have been shipped to the customer, or the services have been rendered. This differs from a cash sale, in which payment is handed over at the same time goods are sold.

When you create an invoice, a journal of the transaction must be created (it's a Sales Journal), so the postings can be transferred to the general ledger. The transaction is posted to all the affected accounts. If you're using accounting software, this is automatic, and many software users don't understand how the journal assigns the transaction to accounts.

As a business owner, you should understand how transactions are posted; otherwise, the data in reports can be confusing. The following examples are presented to clarify the way invoices are journalized as they feed the general ledger.

The journal for a simple sales transaction, involving no inventory or sales tax, is seen in Table 3-1. The posting to Accounts Receivable represents the total amount of the invoice.

Account	Debit	Credit
4000 – Income		100.00
1100 – Accounts Receivable	100.00	

Table 3-1: A journal for a simple sale of goods or services.

If you post certain types of sales to different income accounts as you create the individual items covered by the invoice, the journal for the invoice tracks those income accounts, as seen in Table 3-2.

Account	Debit	Credit
4010 – Income for Services		60.00
4020 – Income for Products		40.00
1100 – Accounts Receivable	100.00	

Table 3-2: Journals reflect all the accounts used in the invoice.

If you're using a divisionalized chart of accounts (explained in Chapter 2), the posting accounts would differ by division. You'd post income to the division that produced the income and track accounts receivable by division. The journal would reflect that by posting the transactions to 4000-02 and 1100-02 if the transaction was generated by the division you'd linked to "02".

When sales tax is involved, it doesn't affect income accounts in the journal (sales tax is neither income nor an expense to the seller). However, the tax affects the total amount due from the customer, which in turn affects the total of Accounts Receivable. The journal displayed in Table 3-3 is based on the fact that services are not taxable, and the products sold are taxable at the rate of 7%.

Account	Debit	Credit
4010 –Income for Services		60.00
4020 – Income for Products Sold		40.00
2200 – Sales Tax Payable		2.80
1100 – Accounts Receivable	102.80	

Table 3-3: The journal includes the sales tax liability.

Things get a bit more complicated when you're selling inventory, because the journal posts the cost of goods sold (usually abbreviated COGS) which is an expense, and decreases the value of your inventory asset. As you can see in Table 3-4, those parts of the overall postings don't affect the amount of the invoice or the sales tax.

Account	Debit	Credit
4000 – Income for Products Sold		40.00
2200 – Sales Tax Payable		2.80
1500 – Inventory Asset		18.00
5000 – COGS	18.00	
1100 – Accounts Receivable	42.80	

Table 3-4: Inventory postings are equal and opposite and don't affect the total amount of the invoice.

NOTE: If you're not using accounting software, you must also reduce the quantity of inventory in your inventory record (accounting software does this automatically).

Customer Invoice Payment Journals

When a customer sends payment for an invoice, you record that payment. The journal for the payment (the Cash Receipts Journal) posts the transaction appropriately. Table 3-5 displays the journal for a customer payment.

Account	Debit	Credit
1000 – Bank Account	42.80	
1100 -Accounts Receivable		42.80

Table 3-5: The invoice payment arrived and the receivables are adjusted.

It's important to understand that an invoice payment journal has no references to the accounts that are tracking income, inventory, or sales tax. All of that information was posted when the original invoice was created.

The payment of the invoice is a second and separate transaction. Many accountants receive questions from clients who want to know why the payment doesn't show what products were sold or what general ledger income accounts were affected. (Those questions are a large motivation for the writing of this book.)

In addition to this journal, which controls the postings to the general ledger, you need to track the customer's activity in the customer's record. You must know the current amount of receivables from each customer. All accounting software does this automatically.

The cash receipts journal does not send anything to the general ledger except the amount of money received. If the original invoice had been $142.80 and $42.80 is paid, the customer's open balance is $100.00 (plus any other unpaid invoices). All of that detailed information is kept in the customer's record.

More information about Accounts Receivable is in Chapter 5 (Managing Assets) and Chapter 11 (Important Reports).

Cash Sales Journals

A cash sale is a transaction in which the customer's money is received at the time the goods or services are received. Don't take the word "cash" literally; the payment may involve cash, a credit card, a debit card, or a gift certificate.

Many companies that do most or all of their business as cash sales don't bother tracking customers for these sales. Some create a single customer (often named "Cash Customers") in their accounting software.

Most accounting software provides a discrete transaction form for cash sales (the name of the form or menu command differs among software programs), and the journal produced by a cash sale (the Cash Receipts Journal) looks similar to Table 3-6.

Account	Debit	Credit
1000 – Bank Account	107.00	
4000 – Income		100.00
2200 – Sales Tax Payable		7.00

Table 3-6: A typical cash sale journal.

Daily Journals from Z-Tapes

Businesses that use a cash register don't record each individual transaction in their books; instead they enter all the daily sales as a batch. Don't forget to create separate entries for taxable items and nontaxable items, and post each line to the appropriate income account (the taxable income account and the nontaxable income account).

Some accounting software (such as QuickBooks and Peachtree) links the sales tax status to an item, and the item is linked to an income account. It's common to link both taxable and nontaxable items to the same income account. The sales tax liability report is generated based on the item information in the sales transaction form, not on the account to which the sale is posted.

Also enter the cash received that you're taking to the bank, which should result in a zero-based transaction. The resulting cash payments journal should look similar to Table 3-7.

Account	Debit	Credit
4010 – Nontaxable Sales		1040.50
4020 – Taxable Sales		2005.50
2200 – Sales Tax Payable		143.54
1000 – Operating Account	3189.54	

Table 3-7: A transaction created from the cash register report.

Of course, it rarely works this well, because when you're ready to take the day's cash receipts to the bank, after you remove the money you want to remain in the till the total in the cash bag doesn't match the total sales (your batch transaction doesn't zero out).

The solution is to track overages or shortages so that the sales match the bank deposit. To track over and short, it's best to create an account named Over/Short of the type Other Income/Expense. Using an income or cost of sales account distorts the gross profit and could effect commission calculations.

> **NOTE**: If you're using software that insists on items
> in the transaction form (such as QuickBooks and
> Peachtree), create over and short items and link them
> to the over/short account.

Enter the over/short amount in the transaction form, using a minus sign for a shortage. (In the transaction journal, an overage posts a credit and a shortage posts a debit.). The transaction journal posts the over/short amount properly, as seen in Table 3-8.

Account	Debit	Credit
4010 – Nontaxable Sales		1050.50
4020 – Taxable Sales		2005.50
2200 – Sales Tax Payable		143.54
7000 – Over & Short	10.00	
1000 – Operating Account	3189.54	

Table 3-8: The transaction total has to match the amount of the bank deposit.

Regardless of the total income, the amount posted to the bank has to match the amount you take to the bank. To make this happen you have to track overages and shortages

Over time, the over/short account usually balances; it's short one day and over another day. However, if you're short every day and the shortages are growing, you have an entirely different problem. You need to look at the person who stands in front of the cash register.

Customer Refunds and Credits

Customer refunds and credits are a fact of business life. Customers return goods or dispute service charges and you have to issue a refund or a credit. In this section I explain how your accounting system posts refunds and credits.

Managing Customer Refunds

Refunds are easy to manage because the refund process is usually a straightforward accounting transaction. Here's what happens:

1. Cash is credited (reduced) and posted to the appropriate cash account.

2. Sales are debited (reduced) and posted to the appropriate income account.

The appropriate cash account depends on the way you deliver the refund:

- If you write a check, and post it to the appropriate income account, the transaction journal posts a debit to income and a credit to the bank account.

- If you take cash from the cash register, include the transaction (using the appropriate income account) in your daily Cash Receipts journal (covered earlier in this chapter). Don't forget to put a note in the cash register so the person creating the daily journal knows about it.

The appropriate income account depends on the method you want to use to track refunds:

- You can post the refund to the same income account you used for the original sale (which reduces total income for that account and displays the net income in reports).

- You can post the refund to another income account you set up specifically to track refunds.

I think it's best to track refunds via a specific account in the income section of your chart of accounts. Name the account Refunds. Because the account is of the type Income, it's called a *contra-sales* account, which means it's an income account and appears in general ledger reports with a negative amount, which reduces total income, but lets you see (and analyze) the effect of refunds on your business.

If sales tax was involved in the original transaction, you must also refund the amount of sales tax to the customer.

If the product the customer returns for the refund is an inventory item, you have to put the item back into inventory. This debits (increases) the inventory asset account, and credits (decreases) the COGS expense that was posted when you sold the inventory.

As an example, Table 3-9 is a transaction journal for a refund by check for a returned inventory item that sold for $160.00. The refund amount is $171.20, including sales tax of $11.20. The COGS of the inventory item is $100.00. (If the refund had been a cash transaction, the credit to cash would have posted to the account linked to the cash register instead of to the bank account).

Account	Debit	Credit
4100 –Refunds	160.00	
2200 – Sales Tax Payable	11.20	
1500 – Inventory Asset	100.00	
5000 – COGS		100.00
1000 – Operating Account		171.20

Table 3-9: Use a separate account to track refunds.

Notice that the inventory asset and COGS are equal and opposite, so they don't affect the amount of the refund (you can think of it as a separate transaction within a transaction, used to manage inventory). The sales tax debit reduces the sales tax payable amount that appears when you create the remittance to the state.

If the inventory was returned because it was damaged, you can't put the item back into inventory. Chapter 8 has information about handling damaged inventory.

Tracking Customer Credits

Customer credits are issued against the customer's current balance by applying the credit to an existing invoice, or by retaining the credit against future purchases (sometimes referred to as a *floating credit*).

Creating Customer Credits

Sometimes the customer wants a credit instead of a refund. Assume the customer is the same as discussed in the previous section on refunds, except that the customer requested a credit.

When you issue a credit instead of a refund, the Accounts Receivable account is credited instead of the bank account.

All accounting software offers a customer credit transaction form, which produces the proper journal, and links the credit to the customer's record. If you're not using accounting software, a customer credit is a reverse invoice, so the journal posts the following transaction:

- Accounts Receivable is credited (reduced).

- The appropriate income account is debited (reduced).

(See the discussion about selecting the appropriate income account in the previous discussion on refunds.)

If the credit involves sales tax and/or inventory products, those postings are also included. You must make sure the customer's record contains the credit, so you can use it against current or future invoices (accounting software does this automatically).

Applying a Customer Credit

Let's look at what happens when the customer uses the credit. Let's assume the customer has an outstanding invoice in the amount of $513.60. The customer sends a check for $342.40 and tells you to apply the credit of $171.20 to make up the difference.

When you complete the task, the transaction journal shows the following postings:

- The bank account is debited for $342.40.

- Accounts Receivable is credited for $342.40

This is another occasion that generates a telephone call from a business owner to an accountant. The question is "I don't understand how a transaction that pays off an invoice for $513.60 doesn't post the amount $513.60 anywhere in my general ledger".

Let's look at what happens when you create an invoice, issue a credit, apply the credit to the invoice, and then apply the customer's payment. Follow the timeline and transactions in Table 3-10 to understand how the accounting works.

Transaction	Account	Debit	Credit	Balance
Invoice created for $513.60	Accounts Receivable	513.60		
	Income		513.60	513.60
.... time passes...				
Credit Created for $171.20	Accounts Receivable		171.20	
	Income	171.20		342.40
... time passes...				
Check for $342.40 is received	Bank	342.40		
	Accounts Receivable		342.40	00.00

Table 3-10: This invoice was paid by credit memo and check.

You can think of the credit that was applied as a payment made by the customer, but that payment wasn't in the form of a check or cash, so it couldn't be deposited in the bank. This means that on the "payment" side of this invoice, no single payment transaction in the amount of $513.60 ever took place. However, during the timeline, the credits to Accounts Receivable (the posting account for payments) add up to $513.60, and that's the amount required to reduce the invoice balance to zero.

Posting Customer Discounts

Customer discounts are commonly applied for one of the following reasons:

- The customer earned a discount for volume purchases or because you're providing a discount for certain customers (such as wholesale customers).

- The customer earned a discount for timely payment of an invoice. The invoice total did not include the discount; instead the discount is applied at the time of payment.

You can post discounts to the same income account you use to post sales, but it's better to create a discrete account for tracking customer discounts. You can then analyze the discounts as a percentage of total sales.

Name the account Discounts Given and put it in the Income section of your chart of accounts. (The reason you name the account Discounts Given instead of Discounts, is that you also may need an account name Discounts Taken to track discounts you receive from vendors; that topic is covered in Chapter 4.)

Applying the Discount to the Sales Transaction

If the discount is applied at the time you create the invoice or cash sale transaction, enter the discount as a line item on the transaction form (using a minus sign because this is a negative number), posting it to the Discounts Given account. The transaction journal makes the postings seen in Table 3-11.

Account	Debit	Credit
4000 – Income		1440.00
4100 – Discounts Given	144.00	
1100 – Accounts Receivable	1296.00	

Table 3-11: Adjust the sales amount by applying a discount.

If your accounting software requires an item for each line of the transaction instead of entering an account (e.g. QuickBooks and Peachtree), a discount item is already configured as a negative number, so you don't enter a minus sign.

Applying the Discount to the Payment

Some businesses (usually manufacturing and distribution companies) provide a discount for timely payment. The vendor (that's you) gives payment terms for the invoice (such as 30 days from the invoice date), and then offers a discount (commonly 2%) if the invoice is paid within a short time (such as within 10 days of the invoice date). The terms data in your invoice form for this type of discount should display as 2%10Net30; your customers know how to interpret that data.

You create the invoice for the full amount without any discount amount indicated. When the customer sends the payment the discount has been taken, so the payment doesn't match the amount of the invoice (or the amount for this customer in Accounts Receivable). When you process the payment, add the discount, using the Discounts Given account.

If the invoice was for $321.00 and the customer took a discount of $6.42, you need to show the invoice as fully paid, but your bank deposit is only $314.58. When you add the discount to the payment transaction, the postings make all of this work properly in the transaction journal, as seen in Table 3-12.

Account	Debit	Credit
1000 – Bank Account	314.58	
4100 – Discounts Given	6.42	
1100 – Accounts Receivable		321.00

Table 3-12: Add the discount to the payment amount.

Most of the time (probably always), customers send a check that takes the discount even if the payment arrives well after the discount date. You can apply the amount of the check to the invoice and leave a balance due, but most companies apply the discount even if the payment is late. This is what we call "goodwill."

Posting Miscellaneous Income

Sometimes you receive income that is unconnected to sales of your services or products. Some examples are interest income, refunds for overpayments to vendors, and rebates from vendors.

Tracking Interest Income

Interest income is treated as part of your company's income for tax purposes, so you need to track it. Create an income account named Interest Income in your chart of accounts. When you create the transaction to put the interest into the bank account, the transaction journal looks like Table 3-13.

Account	Debit	Credit
1000 – Bank Account	5.00	
4200 – Interest Income		5.00

Table 3-13: The transaction increases the bank account and increases interest income.

Tracking Refunds and Rebates Received

Judging by the queries many accountants receive, many business owners don't know how to post a rebate or a refund they receive for an overpayment. Following are some guidelines.

- If the money arrived in the same tax year as the payment was made, you can post the refund/rebate to the original expense you used when you created the payment, or you can post the refund to your Other Income account. (Your accountant may have a preference, so be sure to ask.)

- If the money arrived after the end of your fiscal year, post the refund/rebate to an Other Income account (you don't want to reduce this year's expenses). The reason to use an Other Income account is that your Profit & Loss statement shows Other Income after a subtotal for the current year's ordinary income, and this makes it easier to analyze your "other income" activities.

Chapter 4 has more information on tracking refunds from vendors.

Chapter 4

Tracking Expenses

You have to track your business expenses carefully; otherwise you'll have a difficult time preparing your tax returns, and you also won't be able to analyze the health of your business properly.

An important rule: **Not every check you write is an expense**. You have to understand when to post disbursements to expenses, and when to post them to other types of accounts in your chart of accounts.

This chapter explains the way expenses are posted to your general ledger. Other chapters cover disbursements that are linked to other types of business transactions (assets, liabilities, income (refunds issued), and equity accounts).

Generally, you can define an expense as a product or service you buy from a vendor for the purpose of running your business. You have two ways to pay vendors:

- Enter the bill from the vendor into your accounting system, and then pay the bill (two steps).

- Don't enter the vendor bill; instead, just make the payment (write a check, wire funds, etc.).

Some companies don't enter any vendor bills into their accounting system. They keep bills in a folder and periodically write checks to pay those bills. Some companies only record the bills from vendors if they're not going to pay those bills immediately, or if they plan to make partial payments.

Most companies combine both methods. Many expenses (such as rent, mortgage payments, loan payments, C.O.D. deliveries, etc.) aren't paid in response to a bill; instead you just write a check.

NOTE: Most accounting software provides one command for paying bills that have been entered in the software, and a different command for writing checks to pay vendors whose bills have *not* been entered in the software. Be sure you use the correct function.

Creating Vendors

You have to maintain information about your vendors no matter which payment method you use, and if you're not using accounting software you should set up a vendor record of some sort. You need a single place to retrieve the information you need when you enter and/or pay bills.

Naming Vendors

Every vendor in your system must have a unique name. If you're using accounting software, the vendor setup screen has a field for the vendor name, and then other fields for other information related to that vendor name (company name, address, phone, etc.).

Because each vendor has to be unique, think of the vendor name as the vendor "code" (many accounting software programs actually use the word "code" in the "name this vendor" field so there's absolutely no confusion about the way to use the field).

Other fields in the vendor record provide the vendor's name, address, and so on.

Most businesses have the same vendor for multiple types of payments, and the most common example is a government agency. However, the payments are for unique types of expenses and it's difficult to understand your accounting records if you don't create a separate vendor for each type of payment.

For example, your state's Department of Revenue may be the payee on checks you write for all sorts of payments, such as sales tax remittances, employee withholding of state payroll taxes, unemployment taxes, business income taxes, and so on.

Create a discrete vendor with a vendor code specific to the payment type. To keep your vendor listings for this multi-purpose vendor contiguous, start the vendor name/code with your state abbreviation. For example, you might end up with the following vendors by using these vendor names/codes (this example uses Pennsylvania):

- PABizTax for business income taxes.

- PADOT for payments to the department of transportation.

- PASUTA for state unemployment tax payments.

- PASales for sales tax remittances.

- PAWithhold for withheld employee state income taxes.

In each vendor record, record your state identification number for the particular type of payment (most states assign different ID numbers for different types of payments). In the example presented here, every check uses PA Department of Revenue as the payee when the check is created, and posts the amount to the appropriate account.

Another example is the IRS. Create a separate vendor record for each type of payment. For example, if you have a vendor with the name/code 941 (for federal withholding, social security, and medicare tax payments) and a separate vendor with the name/code 940 (for federal unemployment tax payments), you won't accidentally write a single check or issue a single online payment for both remittances (which the IRS doesn't permit).

If you have multiple telephone lines and receive a separate bill for each line, create a separate vendor for each phone number. This avoids writing a single check for all bills. Use the telephone number as the vendor name/code, and make the telephone company the payee for each payment.

Required Vendor Information

Be sure to have the following information about your vendors available:

- The company name and the correct address for remitting payments. (If you use Purchase Orders for inventory, it's common for the vendor to have one address for receiving POs and a different address for remitting payments.)

- Your account number with the vendor.

- The terms of payment.

- Your credit limit, if one exists.

- A Tax Identification Number (TIN) if the vendor is required to receive Form 1099 from you (covered in Chapter 9).

Optional Vendor Information

In addition, you might want to track additional information about your vendors. The name and telephone number (or e-mail address) of the person in charge of their Accounts Receivable is frequently needed.

You may also find it helpful to assign a Vendor Type to separate your vendors by activity. Some businesses separate the vendors from whom they purchase inventory from vendors for administrative expenses. Other businesses separate subcontractors from other vendors. The way you do business should suggest a way to separate vendors by type. You can create lists and reports of your vendors sorted by type, or exclusively for a specific vendor type.

Tracking Vendor Bills

Entering your bills and then paying them in a separate transaction is accrual accounting. The expense is posted to your general ledger when you enter the bill, not when you pay the bill. If you file taxes on cash basis, your accountant can make the necessary adjustments to the numbers so you only declare the expenses you actually paid.

NOTE: Some accounting software, such as QuickBooks, lets you create reports on either a cash basis or an accrual basis so your accountant doesn't have to make adjustments to the numbers.

Recording a Vendor Bill

When you enter a vendor bill, the transaction amounts are recorded in a Purchases Journal, as seen in Table 4-1. In this case, the vendor bill is for an ordinary business expense, and the other side of the transaction is Accounts Payable.

Account	Debit	Credit
6020 – Telephone	205.50	
2100 – Accounts Payable		205.50

Table 4-1: A typical journal for a bill for an expense.

In addition, the transaction details such as the bill number and the due date should be tracked in the vendor record (accounting software does this automatically).

Sometimes, vendor bills aren't for an expense; some banks send bills for loan payments (loans are liabilities) and other circumstances arise when you receive a bill for another type of payment. However, the majority of vendor bills are for expenses.

Managing Split Transactions

Not all bills fit neatly into one expense account. The bill you receive from your credit card company is a good example, because the line items on the bill probably cover multiple types of expenses. When you have multiple expense account postings for a single bill, the individual lines and their linked accounts are called *the splits*.

Enter each item on the bill separately, posting it to the appropriate expense account, as seen in Table 4-2. The transaction journal tracks the splits, sending each account's posting to the ledger.

If the bill includes multiple postings to the same expense account, you don't have to do the arithmetic before entering the bill into your accounting system. It's easier to follow the line items on the bill to enter the data; as you enter multiple line items posted to the same expense account, the total for each account is posted to the ledger.

Account	Debit	Credit
6100 – Web Hosting Fees	23.95	
6120 – Tech Ref Books	56.92	
6140 – Computer Supplies	80.20	
6250 – Dues & Subscriptions	60.00	
2100 – Accounts Payable		221.07

Table 4-2: The total of the splits equals the amount of the bill.

If you have running balances with any vendor (such as a credit card), enter only the new transactions as each bill arrives, including the new interest. Do *not* enter the amount listed as "Previous balance due"; that's already in your system in Accounts Payable.

Paying Vendor Bills

It's important to understand that there's a difference between making a bill payment and sending a payment to a vendor for whom no bill was entered in your accounting system. These two methods for sending money to vendors are poles apart because they post differently to the general ledger. (Accounting software provides separate commands for these actions.)

- A bill payment is a remittance that pays a bill that has already been entered into your accounting system.

- A remittance to a vendor that is paying a bill that was not entered into your accounting system is called a direct disbursement (and is discussed later in this chapter).

Accountants, bookkeepers, and accounting software support personnel receive many calls from business owners who ask, "I entered a bill and I just paid it, but when I look at the postings for the check I don't see the expenses involved in this bill".

The amounts linked to expense accounts were posted when you entered the bill, and if you want to be reminded about the expenses you have to look at the bill, or look at the postings that went to the ledger from the Purchases Journal.

The payment is a separate transaction that reduces your Accounts Payable and is posted to the ledger from a Cash Payments Journal. If a vendor's bill is entered in your accounting system, paying it produces the postings seen in Table 4-3.

Account	Debit	Credit
1000 – Bank Account		205.50
2100 – Accounts Payable	205.50	

Table 4-3: The Cash Payments Journal.

The posting to Accounts Payable is a debit when you pay the bill, offsetting the credit to Accounts Payable that occurred when you entered the bill. The payment reduces both Accounts Payable and the bank account. If you make a partial payment, the unpaid balance remains in Accounts Payable and on the vendor record.

TIP: When you add up the open payables (balances due) recorded in all the vendor records, the total should always equal the amount in the Accounts Payable account.

Direct Disbursements

A direct disbursement is a payment you make without entering a bill into your accounting system. This is the payment method for those expenses for which vendors don't usually send a bill, such as rent, some loan payments, etc.

It's also the payment method for many small businesses that never enter vendor bills into the system; instead, they store the bills in a folder and create the payments with direct disbursements.

For a direct disbursement, all you have to do is create the check, linking the expense to the appropriate account (or multiple accounts if the bill covers multiple expenses). The check has the postings seen in Table 4-4.

Account	Debit	Credit
1000 – Bank Account		800.00
6000 – Rent	800.00	

Table 4-4: A direct disbursement removes funds from the bank and increases expenses.

Many accountants have seen client records for bills and checks entered on the same date, because the client invented a bill in order to send money to a vendor. These clients either didn't understand that a direct disbursement is available or they are using accounting software that doesn't allow the direct disbursement method.

The advantage of a direct disbursement over entering a bill and then paying it is that it's less data entry; you have one transaction instead of two.

The disadvantage of a direct disbursement is the inability to track balances due if you make a partial payment. You have to wait until the next bill arrives from the vendor, you have to hope your partial payment arrived in time to be displayed on the next bill, and you have to hope the vendor's arithmetic is correct.

Tracking Electronic Payments

Today, businesses write fewer checks than they used to (in fact, some businesses almost never use a physical check). It's faster, easier, and cheaper (no envelope, no stamp) to use electronic transfers to move money from your checking account to the vendor's bank account.

When you pay vendors via electronic transfer, you enter the transaction in your accounting system exactly the same way you'd enter a payment made by check. The only difference is the lack of a check number.

You can use a "code" as a check number when you enter the transaction in your accounting system. Some people use EFT (Electronic Funds Transfer), some use ACH (Automated Clearing House – a network that transfers money among banks in the United States), and some omit the check number field, leaving it blank. There's no particular advantage or disadvantage to any of these choices.

You have a variety of ways to create electronic vendor payments:

- Let the vendor reach into your bank account and withdraw the payment (you have to fill out a permission form online or via paper).

- Set up an electronic transfer with your bank to transfer the money from your account to your vendor's account. Many banks provide this service on their websites, as part of their Bill Pay features.

- Sign up for ACH file processing with your bank (if your bank offers this service) and fill out forms on the bank's website to send multiple electronic payments as a batch.

- Buy ACH software that lets you create ACH files directly from your accounting software or from a spreadsheet, and upload the file to the software company (or directly to your bank if the software is designed for that function) to move the payments through the banking system.

If you have access to ACH file processes through your bank or through a software service, one ACH file can contain transfers in both directions. That means you can use a single ACH file to take money due to you from a customer's bank account and deposit it into your bank account (with the customer's permission, of course), and to take money from your bank account and deposit it into a vendor's bank account.

Online Bill Payments Through Your Bank

Most banks offer online bill payments to business customers via a web page. The bank provides a login name, you create a password, and then you log in to the online banking web page. You have to create your vendor list on the web page, including vendor address information and your customer number with the vendor. Then you can issue payments to those vendors from the web page.

If you have accounting software that provides online banking (and your bank supports your software's online banking feature), you can create payments in the software, mark them as "Online Payments" and then upload them to the bank.

If the vendor is registered in the database for E-Pay payments (a national database that banks have access to), the bank sends an electronic transfer. If the vendor is not registered in the ACH database, the bank creates a check and mails it to your vendor.

Some banks offer ACH services for their online bill paying service. If you provide the vendor's bank information in your online vendor setup, the bank will transfer the funds directly from your account to the vendor's account instead of mailing a check.

If you create the payments within your accounting software, your ACH information on the bank's website is not checked by the software and vendors who are not in the national E-Pay database will be mailed physical checks.

How Banks Manage Online Payments

When you send a regular check to a vendor, the money isn't removed from your bank account until the check is presented to your bank for payment by the vendor's bank. This means the payee has received, endorsed, and deposited the check.

When you send an online payment through your bank, the money is immediately removed from your checking account and placed into the bank's checking account.

When you view your bank transactions on the bank's website, on your statement, or through an online banking connection with your accounting software, you see the deduction for the online payment. However, unlike deductions you see for the checks you create and send, this doesn't mean that the vendor has received and deposited your payment; instead it means the bank has moved the money from your account to its account.

The bank sends a check to the payee from its own account, and after the vendor deposits it the check is sent to the bank's checking account for payment and clearance (after all, it's the bank's check, not your check). No notification is sent to you when the check is presented for payment.

If you create an online payment that is an electronic transfer, the same process applies; that is, the money is removed from your account before the electronic payment is transmitted, and the transmission is from the bank's bank account.

When you get your statement from the bank, you don't see physical checks or pictures of checks (depending on the way your bank sends you checks with the statement) that were online payments. Those checks are sent to, and retained by, the bank (because it's the bank's checking account that processed the check).

If you create and mail your own checks, when a vendor calls to say that the check wasn't received, you can check with your bank to see if the check cleared. If it didn't clear, you can stop payment and issue a new check. If it cleared, you can request a copy of the back of the check in order to see the endorsement. When you send the endorsement information to the vendor the vendor can correct its records to apply your payment. If the vendor claims the endorsement is bogus, your bank has procedures for recovering the funds and you can send another check to the vendor.

It's not quite as straightforward when the check is an online payment, but your bank has procedures that cover this situation.

If an online payment check is not presented for payment to the bank's bank account within some number of days (usually 90 days), a flag goes up in the bank's software. The money is automatically returned to your bank account, and a "stop payment" order is issued from the bank's bank account (not your bank account).

Ninety days is a long time, and well before this automatic stop payment is issued, you're going to hear from the vendor. You have to remit payment immediately. Go to your bank and explain the problem.

If the bank finds that the check it sent was presented for payment, the procedures are the same as if this happened with your own check. The bank will provide a picture of the check, including the endorsement, which you can send to the vendor. The vendor will either discover its mistake in entering your payment, or will claim the endorsement is bogus (and the same remedies are available as for your own checks that have forged endorsements).

If the check has not cleared, your bank should offer you the following options:

- The bank will reissue the check and send it to the payee using the funds that were removed for the original payment. The money doesn't have to be withdrawn from your account again because the bank still has it, since the check wasn't presented for payment by the payee's bank. (Most banks call you or the vendor to check the vendor's address in case a bad address is the problem; if so, the check is reissued to the corrected address.)

- The bank will return the money to your account so you can issue your own check (or make other payment arrangements) to the vendor.

A few banks, mostly large national banks, actually print a check that comes from your account. That check clears your bank the way it would if you'd written the check; that is, the check clears after the vendor deposits it and the check is sent to your bank. Most of these banks charge fees for online banking. Before signing up for this service, do the arithmetic: Do you send enough checks to make the bank's fee a bargain when compared to the cost of postage?

Tracking Vendor Credits

If you return a product, a dispute over service fees, or inadvertently overpay a vendor, the vendor may issue a credit. You use this credit against existing or future bills, so you must record the credit in your system.

Creating a Vendor Credit

A credit from a vendor is a reverse purchase, and your transaction reflects that fact. Create the transaction using the same expense account you used when you created the original transaction, using a negative amount (a minus sign). The resulting transaction journal looks like Table 4-5.

Account	Debit	Credit
6500 – Printing		400.00
2100 – Accounts Payable	400.00	

Table 4-5: This credit removes the original expense and decreases A/P.

NOTE: If you're using accounting software, there may be a specific form for vendor credits. In that case, you probably don't have to use a negative number.

Be sure you enter the information in the vendor record, so you can use the credit against existing or future bills. If you're using accounting software, the transfer of this information into the vendor record is automatic.

Applying a Vendor Credit to a Bill

Eventually, you apply a vendor credit to an outstanding bill from the vendor. This means the amount of money that comes out of your bank account when you create the payment is less than the amount of the bill; the difference is paid off by the credit.

If you returned an inventory product to the vendor, the process is a bit more complicated. You have to post the amounts that affect inventory and you have to decrease the quantity of your inventory items. Inventory returns are discussed in Chapter 8.

Managing Vendor Refunds

If a vendor elects to send a refund instead of a credit, entering the refund into your accounting system is easier than tracking vendor credits. A refund doesn't affect the current balance due, doesn't affect your A/P balance, and isn't used in reducing the amount of future bills from the vendor.

A vendor refund is money that can be treated either as income or a reduction of an expense that you previously paid. You have two methods for posting this transaction:

- Post the money (a bank deposit) to an account named "Other Income".

- Post the money (a bank deposit) to the original expense account you used when you paid the original bill.

Ask your accountant which method is preferred. If the refund arrived after the end of your fiscal year, and the original payment was in the previous fiscal year, use the Other Income account so you don't skew the current year expenses in your Profit & Loss statement.

Table 4-6 shows the transaction journal for a refund that is posted to the Other Income account.

Account	Debit	Credit
1000 – Bank Account	100.00	
7000 – Other Income		100.00

Table 4-6: This refund increased the amount in the
bank account and the amount of Other
Income received.

Petty Cash Expenses

Accountants frequently receive questions about how to handle
cash layouts for business expenses. Usually, the questions
involve one of the following scenarios:

- Someone used cash or a personal credit card to
  buy something for the company and that person
  needs to be reimbursed.

- Someone used the debit card for the business
  account to withdraw cash and didn't use all of that
  cash for a business expense; the remaining cash
  needs to be tracked.

- Someone is going to be traveling for the company
  and needs cash in advance (and will need to return
  unspent cash).

There are other scenarios similar to these, but the ultimate
question is, "How do I manage cash transactions that fall outside
of the usual data entry for vendor bills and payments"?

The best solution is to have a cash box, a metal box that
locks in which you keep a certain amount of cash. Then, you
track the cash that goes in and out of the box by creating a
petty cash account in your chart of accounts. This account
treated like a bank account. (If you're using accounting

software, the Account Type is "Bank".) Here's how a petty cash box works:

1. You put money in it.

2. You account for the money that's disbursed.

3. When almost all the money is spent you replenish the money in the box.

The petty cash account in your accounting system doesn't represent a real bank account; it just represents the money that moved from the real bank account into the cash box.

Filling the Cash Box

You have to put money into the cash box, both literally (get cash) and figuratively (record a withdrawal from your bank account to your petty cash account). Most of the time the cash box is filled the first time by writing a check to Cash from your bank account, cashing the check at the bank, and bringing the cash back to the box. The check should be in the amount you want to use as the "base amount" for incidental cash expenses.

When you create the check in the bank account in your accounting system, post the check to the Petty Cash account you created. You don't post a petty cash check to an expense; instead the expense postings are recorded when you disburse cash from the box.

The transaction journal credits (reduces) the bank account and debits (increases) the petty cash account, as seen in Table 4-7.

Account	Debit	Credit
1000 – Bank Account		100.00
1020 – Petty Cash	100.00	

Table 4-7: Putting money into the petty cash box is like a transfer of funds between banks.

Recording Petty Cash Disbursements

As you take cash out of the petty cash box in the office, you must record those disbursements in the petty cash account in your accounting system.

Make it a hard and fast rule that nobody receives cash for reimbursement without a receipt, and store the receipts in a large envelope marked with the current tax year (e.g. Cash Payments 2010). Store the envelope with your tax return, just in case you hear from an auditor.

Tracking Petty Cash Disbursements for Expenses

When you provide petty cash to someone who needs to be reimbursed for purchases, record those disbursements in the petty cash account (*not* in the bank account; the bank account is for expense reimbursements that are provided by a check). Make sure you have a receipt that indicates the details of the purchase.

If you're using accounting software, create a check in your petty cash account (which is a fake check, of course) and post it to the appropriate expense account. If the software automatically inserts a check number, you can change the number it to the word "cash", delete the number, or accept the number (because you're never going to get a bank statement and have to reconcile this account, the check number reference doesn't matter).

When you record a petty cash disbursement, you usually don't need to enter a vendor name (because these expenses usually don't have to be tracked the way you track vendors that send bills and for whom you need to keep a history). If you wish, you can create a single vendor named PettyCash for all petty cash disbursements.

You can keep the receipts in the cash box and create the fake check transaction weekly (or even monthly if you don't have a lot of cash disbursements). Just create a line item for each expense and post the total for that expense. Mark the receipt "ENTERED" and move it to your "cash payments" envelope when you've posted the receipt to your accounting system.

Tracking Petty Cash Advances

You have to track advances you disburse from the cash box so that the petty cash account in your accounting system always matches the amount of cash in the box. However, advances for future expenses aren't expenses (yet), so they have to be posted differently.

Create an account of the type Other Current Asset, and name it Petty Cash Advances. If you're using numbered accounts, select a number in the appropriate range for Other Current Asset.

When someone needs a cash advance, perform both of the following steps:

1. Have the person sign an IOU that says he or she took $XX.XX dollars. Put the IOU in the cash box, and disburse the money.

2. Enter the transaction in your accounting system, using a fake check from your petty cash fake bank account. Post the transaction to the account named Petty Cash Advances.

When the person who took the advance spends the money, one of the following scenarios occurs:

- More than the advance was spent and the person has receipts for the entire amount spent (the advance and the additional out-of-pocket expenses).

- Less than the advance was spent and the person has receipts for the spent amount and has the left over cash.

- The money spent is exactly equal to the amount of the advance (it almost never works this way).

The best way to manage moving the advanced monies out of the Petty Cash Advances account and into the appropriate expense account(s) is to create a journal entry. You have a choice of two methods for doing this, and you should choose the one that's easiest and least confusing for you.

- You can move all the advanced funds back into the Petty Cash account (essentially voiding the IOU), and then create your disbursements from within the Petty Cash account as described earlier for tracking disbursements for expenses.

- You can include all the postings to expenses in addition to the return of any advanced funds in a single journal entry.

Note that no matter which way you enter the transaction, you are only tracking the money advanced to this person.

There may be additional money in the Petty Cash Advances account representing other advances to other people. You are not emptying the Petty Cash Advances account; you are only moving the funds for this particular advance.

Let's say the advance was for $100.00. If you want to move the funds back into the Petty Cash account and create the transactions to cover the disbursements separately, create the journal entry seen in Table 4-8.

Account	Debit	Credit
1020 – Petty Cash (ersatz bank account)	100.00	
1300 – Petty Cash Advances		100.00

Table 4-8: Return the money to the Petty Cash account and post the expenses in a separate journal entry.

If you want to perform both tasks (removing the advance and posting the disbursements) in one journal entry, Table 4-9 provides a sample transaction for the scenario in which the person spent $120.00 ($20.00 of her own money in addition to the $100.00 advanced) and has receipts. This transaction moves funds directly from the Petty Cash Advances account to the appropriate expense accounts, and then takes the additional money spent from the Petty Cash account (because you have to give additional cash to the person from the cash box).

Account	Debit	Credit
1300 – Petty Cash Advances		100.00
6200 – Tolls & Parking	50.00	
6150 – Office Supplies	40.00	
6220 – Meals	30.00	
1020 – Petty Cash		20.00

Table 4-9: This journal entry changes the money that was advanced into expenses.

If the person spent less than the advance, and is returning money to the petty cash box, your journal entry must reflect that fact, as seen in Table 4-10. This transaction moves funds directly from the Petty Cash Advances account to the expenses, and puts the leftover cash back into the Petty Cash account (reflecting the fact that you actually put money back into the cash box).

Account	Debit	Credit
1300 – Petty Cash Advances		100.00
6200 – Tolls & Parking	20.00	
6150 – Office Supplies	20.00	
6220 – Meals	30.00	
1020 – Petty Cash	30.00	

Table 4-10: Remove the advance and dispense it to expenses along with the cash returned to petty cash.

If the person spent exactly the amount advanced, then you remove the money from the Petty Cash Advances account and post the expenses (see Table 4-11). Since no money is returned to the cash box nor is more money taken from the cash box, the Petty Cash account isn't included in the transaction.

Account	Debit	Credit
1300 – Petty Cash Advances		100.00
6200 – Tolls & Parking	30.00	
6150 – Office Supplies	40.00	
6220 – Meals	30.00	

Table 4-11: Move the money out of the Petty Cash Advances account and into expense accounts.

Re-filling the Cash Box

As you dispense cash from the cash box, you need to replace it. The usual method is to bring the cash box back to its original balance (the amount of the first check you wrote to petty cash). Use the same steps you used to write the first check to petty cash, using the total amount of funds disbursed as the amount of the check. This brings the total available in the cash box back to the original amount.

You can write the check for less than the disbursed funds if you determine that you were putting too much money in the cash box, or you can write the check for more than the disbursed funds if you think you need to increase the amount of cash available in the cash box.

Tracking Debit Cards

Many accountants find that business owners who have a debit card attached to their business bank account are confused about the way to enter debit card transactions. There are two types of debit card transactions:

- The debit card is used at the cash register of a retail store to pay for a purchase.

- The debit card is used to withdraw cash from an ATM and the cash remains in the pocket of the person who withdrew it until it's spent for business expenses (which can take days or weeks). Some business owners call this "walking around money".

A debit card withdrawal from your bank account is no different from a check you write or an automatic deduction by a vendor. A withdrawal is a withdrawal, no matter what form it takes. You have to enter every withdrawal from your bank account into your accounting system so you know your current bank balance, and so you can reconcile the bank account.

If the debit card is used at a retail location to pay for a purchase, entering the transaction is easy; essentially it's a check with no number (because there's no physical check) and it's posted to the appropriate expense account. You may want to use DM (for debit memo), ATM, or another reference in place of the check number, depending on the way these transactions are noted on your bank statements. The resulting transaction journal resembles Table 4-12.

Account	Debit	Credit
1000 – Bank Account		80.00
6150 – Office Supplies	80.00	

Table 4-12: The transaction journal for a debit card withdrawal is the same as the transaction journal for a check.

If the debit card is used to withdraw cash that isn't spent immediately, it's more complicated. You must remove the money from the bank account, but there aren't any expenses to post. How do you accomplish this?

The process is similar to the process used for advances out of the petty cash box, described in the previous section. This is money owed to the company, and it has to be tracked (money owed to the company is an asset).

Some businesses tell people who withdraw money from the bank at an ATM that the cash has to be brought back to the office and put into the petty cash box. Then it can be withdrawn from petty cash as needed and posted to the appropriate expenses.

If you adopt this policy the transaction is easy to enter; just post the fake check to the Petty Cash account (which is treated like a bank account, as explained earlier). In fact, this is a way to fill the petty cash box without writing a real check and sending someone to the bank to cash it. The transaction journal looks like Table 4-13.

Account	Debit	Credit
1000 – Bank Account		80.00
1020 – Petty Cash Account	80.00	

Table 4-13: You can use a debit card at an ATM to put cash into the petty cash box.

TIP: If your accounting software has a Transfer Funds Between Banks feature, use that transaction form to move the money. Because the Petty Cash account is set up as a bank, this works beautifully.

Unfortunately, it's frequently the business owner who is the person who uses the debit card to get cash, and business owners frequently choose to ignore the rules. In that case, tracking the withdrawn cash is more complicated.

The only way to remove the cash from the bank and track its use is to follow the instructions in the previous section for tracking advances of petty cash. You need to post the transaction to an asset account and then use a journal entry to move it from the asset account to the appropriate expense as the money is spent.

If you have a petty cash box, and you also have people withdrawing money from the bank with a debit card, you should set up a separate Other Current Asset account for these ATM withdrawals. This is much less confusing than trying to track the petty cash box and the debit card withdrawal from one asset account. Name the account "Bank Funds Held in Cash" or "Walking Around Money" or whatever seems logical. Then, as the money is spent, use a journal entry to move the expended funds into expense accounts, as seen in Table 4-14.

Account	Debit	Credit
1350 – Bank Funds Held in Cash		80.00
6200 – Tolls & Parking	25.00	
6150 – Office Supplies	40.00	
6220 – Meals	15.00	

Table 4-14: As the withdrawn money is spent, move the spent funds out of the asset account that's tracking the cash into the appropriate expense accounts.

Chapter 5

Managing Assets

• •

An asset is something your business owns that has value or usefulness. In accounting, assets are categorized and sub-categorized by various definitions.

Chapter 1 contains a complete list of all the asset categories, and in this chapter I'll discuss the asset categories you commonly encounter as you track business activities.

Tracking Cash

Don't take the word "cash" literally; in accounting it means the money in your bank account(s) as well as cash that's in a cash register till or a petty cash box. Most of the transactions that take place as you run your business involve cash: You move money in and out of your cash accounts as you track sales and expenses.

Earlier chapters in this book discussed the income and expense transactions that affect your cash accounts (selling to customers and buying from vendors). In this section I'll go over some of the additional transaction types and tasks that involve tracking cash.

Transferring Money Between Accounts

It's common to move money between bank accounts. Most businesses with more than a couple of employees maintain an account for payroll, and transfer money from the operating account into the payroll account just before each payday.

TIP: If you outsource your payroll, you should have a separate payroll account. Many payroll services reach into your bank account to create paychecks, remit liabilities, and pay employer expenses. The payroll company shouldn't have access to your operating account.

Some businesses move money that won't be needed immediately from the operating account into a money market account to get interest. Some businesses deposit all their income into a money market account, and then move funds into the operating account as the funds are needed to cover expenses.

Creating a Transfer Transaction

The process of transferring funds is essentially "write a check from the sending account and deposit it into the receiving account".

If you have the ability to transfer funds electronically, you can use a transaction that involves a fake check (a check with no number that never physically exists). Call the bank or use the bank's online services to effect the transfer and then create the transaction with the fake check; instead of a check number, you can use "EFT" (electronic funds transfer) for the transfer's reference number.

If the accounts are in separate banks and you can't transfer the funds electronically, or the bank charges too much to transfer funds to another bank, create the transaction with a real check and deposit it into the receiving bank.

If you're using accounting software, the transaction you create is a simple one-step process: Post the check to the receiving bank account. The software automatically creates the transaction in both banks, producing the transaction journal seen in Table 5-1 (in this case, a transfer from the operating account to the payroll account).

Account	Debit	Credit
1000 – Bank Account		3000.00
1010 – Payroll Account	3000.00	

Table 5-1: A transfer between bank accounts credits (reduces) the sending account and debits (increases) the receiving account.

If you're using a manual system or a spreadsheet, you need to create both sides of the transaction separately in order to maintain the bank transaction lists so they match the monthly bank statements.

1. In the sending bank, create the check and post it to an account named Funds Transfer. If that account doesn't exist you must create it; the account is an asset account with the account type Bank (the same type as your bank accounts).

2. In the receiving bank, create a deposit (not a sale, this is not income) and post it to the Funds Transfer account.

In Step 1 you credited the sending bank and debited the Funds Transfer account. In Step 2 you credited the Funds Transfer account (bringing it to zero) and debited the receiving bank.

NOTE: Another cash asset that you need to track is petty cash, which is the cash you keep on hand (either in a cash box or in a cash register till) to cover cash expenses. Tracking petty cash is covered in Chapter 4.

Tracking Accounts Receivable

Accounts receivable is the accounting terminology for money owed to you, and it's often abbreviated as *A/R*. (In the business community, the common jargon for A/R is *money on the street*).

A/R increases when you deliver a service or a product and send an invoice to the customer, and the customer hasn't yet remitted payment. This is an asset because, as I explained in Chapter 1, an asset is something that you own or something that belongs to you, even if you don't have it in your possession at the moment.

NOTE: Some companies (usually retail businesses) never have an A/R balance because the customer always pays for purchases at the time the sale takes place.

A/R postings take place whenever the amount of money owed to you changes:

- A/R is debited (increased) when you create an invoice.

- A/R is credited (decreased) when you receive a payment on an invoice or issue a credit to a customer.

Increases to Accounts Receivable

If you create an invoice for $100.00, the posting journal (a sales journal) resembles the transaction journal seen in Table 5-2.

Account	Debit	Credit
4000 – Income		100.00
1100 – Accounts Receivable	100.00	

Table 5-2: Creating an invoice posts the amount of the invoice to A/R.

It's important to know that the entire amount of the invoice is posted to A/R, even if the amount includes items other than sales/income. For example, the sales tax you charge is not income, so while the A/R account posts the total amount of the transaction, the postings on the "other side" of A/R are made to multiple accounts, as illustrated in Table 5-3.

Account	Debit	Credit
4000 – Income		100.00
2100 – Sales Tax Payable		7.00
1100 – Accounts Receivable	107.00	

Table 5-3: Sales tax is included in the amount posted to A/R.

Decreases to Accounts Receivable

Accounts Receivable is decreased whenever the amount of money owed to you is reduced by one of the following actions:

- The customer sends a payment for an invoice (covered next).

- You issue a credit to a customer with an A/R balance (covered in Chapter 3).

Receiving Payments on Invoices

When a customer sends a payment for an invoice that's in your accounting system, the payment reduces the A/R balance and increases the bank account in which you deposit the payment. For example, a payment of $100.00 is posted as seen in Table 5-4.

Account	Debit	Credit
1000 – Bank Account	100.00	
1100 – Accounts Receivable		100.00

Table 5-4: The journal for a customer payment is simple and straightforward.

The invoice for which the payment is received may be larger than the amount of the payment. If the original invoice was for $200.00 and the customer sends a partial payment of $100.00, the A/R balance is reduced by $100.00. The remaining balance of $100.00 remains in A/R.

When you view a customer's A/R report, as illustrated in Table 5-5 (along with the postings), you can see the way A/R changes over the course of time.

NOTE: A/R is also decreased when you create a customer credit, or apply a discount to an invoice. Those transactions are covered in Chapter 3.

In accounting, we "prove" the accounts receivable total by adding up the outstanding balances for each customer and making sure the total matches the current balance of the accounts receivable account.

If you have accounting software an Accounts Receivable report is available and is usually called the *A/R Aging Report*. The report can be configured to show intervals, such as the total due that is 30 days old, 60 days old, and 90 or more days old. Match the grand total against the A/R asset total on the balance sheet. (If it doesn't match, be sure you're using the same date on both reports.)

If you're not using accounting software you must keep a running total of the open balance due for each customer so you can match the grand total of all customer balances against the total in the A/R account.

Date	Transaction	Account	Debit	Credit
3/30/2010	Invoice #111	1100– Accounts Receivable	200.00	
3/30/2010		4000 – Income		200.00
4/15/2010	Paymt on Inv #111	1100 – Accounts Receivable		100.00
4/15/2010		1000 – Bank Account	100.00	
4/30/2010	Invoice #123	1100 – Accounts Receivable	300.00	
4/30/2010		4000 – Income		300.00
5/15/2010	Paymt on Inv #111-123	1100 – Accounts Receivable		200.00
5/15/2010		1000 – Bank Account	200.00	
	A/R Balance		**200.00**	

Table 5-5: The A/R balance is a running record of the debits and credits.

Writing Off Receivables You'll Never Collect

Sometimes you have customers that aren't going to pay you. They may have gone out of business, they may have serious financial difficulties that seem to be permanent, or they may just be deadbeats.

At some point you and your accountant will decide you no longer want to show the uncollectible amount as an asset on your balance sheet. The way you perform this task depends on the way you file taxes:

- If you file taxes on an accrual basis you may be able to write off the amount as an expense to an account named *bad debt expense*.

- If you file taxes on a cash basis, create a customer credit for the uncollectible amount and apply it to the uncollectible open invoice(s). The invoice balance(s), and the A/R balance for the customer, are zeroed out.

If you file taxes on cash basis instead of accrual, there's no such thing as a bad debt. Many business owners assume that every uncollectible customer balance can be posted to the Profit & Loss statement as a bad debt expense, but that's an incorrect assumption. After all, in cash basis reporting you didn't recognize the income from the unpaid invoice, and if the income doesn't exist for tax purposes how can you have a tax deductible bad debt expense? Use a customer credit to reduce A/R and get rid of the uncollectible amount.

Bad Debt Expense

If you file taxes on the accrual basis the income was recognized and reported, so you may be able to use a bad debt expense to reverse the income you recognized but never received. To accomplish this, you need an expense account named Bad Debt Expense.

When you and your accountant agree that it's appropriate to post a bad debt expense, ask your accountant to give you the transactions needed to move the unpaid amount to your Bad Debt Expense account and clear the customer balance so it no longer appears in A/R.

There are no step-by-step instructions I can provide because your company structure, the accounting software you're using (if you're using software), the age of the bad debt, and other circumstances determine the way a bad debt transaction is created. Remember, it's not enough to post an amount to the Bad Debt Expense account; you must also clear the customer's A/R balance.

GAAP (Generally Accepted Accounting Principles) rules say that if you're on the accrual basis, you should create and maintain a reserve for uncollectible customer accounts. This reserve is held in an account named Allowance for Doubtful Accounts, which is an Accounts Receivable type of account. Many small businesses don't use an Allowance for Doubtful Accounts account. You should ask your accountant whether it's needed for your business, and have him or her show you how to use it.

Don't let your accountant make journal entries against A/R to apply credits or write off open balances for specific customers. A/R changes should be made by creating transactions that are linked to the customer(s) in question. Have your accountant explain what has to be done and then create the appropriate transaction for the customer. The only acceptable journal entry against A/R is the year-end entry to provide a cash-basis report for tax preparation, and that journal entry must be reversed the next day (the first day of the next fiscal year).

Tracking Loans Owed To You

Your business may loan money to an individual (including you), another business, or an employee. You need to track the loan balance as well as the interest you're collecting on the loan.

When your business provides a loan to someone, it's an asset because the money belongs to your business (your business is the *creditor* and the recipient of the loan is the *debtor*.)

Creating the Loan

To track a loan you've made to someone, create an account of the type Current Asset for the loan and create a Customer account for the debtor. When you write the check to the debtor, post the check to the loan asset account, as seen in Table 5-6.

Account	Debit	Credit
1000 – Bank Account		3000.00
1310 – Loan to P.Goodman	3000.00	

Table 5-6: A loan you make isn't an expense, it's an asset.

If you extend the loan over multiple checks instead of writing one large check, each check is posted the same way.

Sending Loan Payment Invoices

You can, if you wish, send invoices to the debtor for each payment due. The invoice posts the transaction to the loan asset account, as seen in Table 5-7.

Account	Debit	Credit
1100 – Accounts Receivable	300.00	
1310 – Loan to P.Goodman		300.00

Table 5-7: Sending an invoice reduces the amount owed on the loan.

If you're charging interest, the amount due for interest does not post to the loan asset (the principal); instead it posts to an income account named Interest Income as seen in Table 5-8.

Account	Debit	Credit
1100 – Accounts Receivable	309.00	
4900 – Interest Income		9.00
1310 – Loan to P.Goodman		300.00

Table 5-8: Interest you charge on a loan is income.

Receiving Loan Payments

As the debtor pays back the loan, create a cash receipt transaction for the payment. If you don't create invoices (instead, the payment arrives automatically), the postings are illustrated in Table 5-9. Note that this table includes posting for interest; if you're not charging interest eliminate the interest amount.

Account	Debit	Credit
1000 – Bank Account	309.00	
4900 – Interest Income		9.00
1310 – Loan to P.Goodman		300.00

Table 5-9: When a payment arrives that was not invoiced, it's posted to the loan asset to reduce the principal.

If you sent an invoice the postings differ, as seen in Table 5-10. When you receive payment on an invoice, don't post amounts to the loan principal or the interest; that was accomplished when you created the invoice.

Account	Debit	Credit
1000 – Bank Account	309.00	
1110 – Accounts Receivable		309.00

Table 5-10: Invoice payments reduce A/R and increase the bank account.

NOTE: If the loan is to an employee and you want to deduct payments from the employee's paycheck, configure the payment as an after-tax payroll deduction that is posted to the loan's asset account.

Vendor Deposits and Prepaid Expenses

It's not uncommon to face the requirement of an upfront deposit on some services such as rent or utilities. The deposits are usually held for a certain time, and then are either returned to you or applied as a credit to your balance by the vendor.

Sometimes, vendors want you to prepay all or part of an expense you're incurring. Prepaid expenses are usually tracked under the following circumstances:

- Some vendors may ask for a prepayment on a large order if you don't have a purchase history with the vendor.

- Some expenses (e.g. insurance) may require an annual or semi-annual payment that your accountant wants to expense one month at a time.

The funds you remit for any of these transactions fall into the definition of an asset: "It's your money even though someone else is holding it." To track these remittances you have to create an asset account for Deposits Held by Others and/or an asset account for Prepaid Expenses. Both of these are defined as Current Assets.

The reason I suggest naming the asset account Deposits Held by Others is to make sure you don't confuse it with accounts that track deposits you're holding for customers, such as prepayments on orders, retainers, or other customer monies you're holding (which are liabilities). Naming an account "Deposits" or "Deposits Held" may be confusing; deposits to whom, from whom?

Tracking Deposits Sent to Vendors

Sending a deposit to a vendor is usually a straightforward transaction; you merely write a check. However, the check isn't an expense, it's an asset. Therefore, you post it to the Vendor Deposits asset account to create the transaction journal seen in Table 5-11. The payee could be the landlord, a utility company, or any other vendor who requires a deposit.

Account	Debit	Credit
1000 – Bank Account		800.00
1310 – Deposits Held by Others	800.00	

Table 5-11: This check isn't an expense, it's an asset.

Returns of Vendor Deposits

Usually vendors return your deposit after a certain period of time. The common method for returning a deposit is to send you a check, but sometimes the vendor may apply the deposit against the next bill.

If you receive a check, all you have to do is deposit the check into your bank account and post the transaction to the Deposits Held by Others asset account. This creates a transaction journal that is the reverse of the journal that recorded the check you wrote for the deposit.

- Your bank account is debited (increased).

- The asset account is credited (decreased).

95

If the vendor gives you a credit against the current expense (the amount due to the vendor) instead of sending you a check, you have to turn the asset into an expense. The method you use for this action is a journal entry, as seen in Table 5-12.

Account	Debit	Credit
6000 – Rent	800.00	
1310 – Deposits Held by Others		800.00

Table 5-12: Change the asset to an expense with a journal entry.

If the amount of the deposit that's applied to the next bill is less than the amount of the bill, you have to write a check for the open balance. The check is posted to the appropriate expense, not to the Deposits Held by Others asset account. The total of the returned deposit and the check amount equals the expense that's posted for the month.

Tracking Prepaid Expenses

If you pay in advance when you purchase goods or services from a vendor, that payment is an asset. Create a Current Asset account named Prepaid Expenses to track these transactions.

When you create the check for the prepaid expense, post it to the Prepaid Expenses account. This credits (decreases) the amount in the bank account and debits (increases) the amount in the Prepaid Expenses account.

To turn the asset into an expense when the vendor's bill arrives (which may have a zero balance if your deposit was payment in full), create a journal entry that credits (decreases) the Prepaid Expenses account for the amount of your prepayment and debits (increases) the appropriate Expense account. Now you have an expense on the books.

If there are additional charges on the vendor's bill (such as shipping costs, or the balance due if your advance payment was not for the entire amount), pay those charges the way you usually pay bills, posting the amount to the appropriate expense account.

Allocating Yearly Payments to Monthly Expenses

If you pay an annual fee for a service that's provided monthly (such as insurance, security services, technical support contracts, etc.), your accountant may want you to track the expense on a monthly basis.

In this scenario, when you write the single check for the annual fee to the vendor, post it to the Prepaid Expenses asset account, not to an expense account. You then post the expense by creating a journal entry each month similar to the one seen in Table 5-13, which is the monthly expense for an annual premium of $1200.00. The journal entry reduces the Prepaid Expenses asset account and increases the expense account.

Date	Account	Debit	Credit
5/01/2010	8550 - Insurance	100.00	
5/01/2010	1320 – Prepaid Expenses		100.00

Table 5-13: This entry applies the current month's insurance cost to the Insurance expense.

Inventory Asset

The value of your inventory asset is the total costs expended for all inventory currently in stock (the current quantity on hand) including purchases from vendors, payments to freight delivery to your facility, labor paid on items you manufacture for sale, and other costs included in your manufacturing process. This means the asset value changes often, because you receive and ship inventory constantly. Inventory is a Current Asset.

The bookkeeping tasks involved in tracking inventory are not as straightforward as the tasks involved in creating sales or purchasing non-inventory goods and services. Therefore, I've devoted a separate chapter to the subject; read Chapter 8 to learn how to enter inventory related transactions.

Fixed Assets

A fixed asset is something that a business owns and uses to run the business and produce income. Fixed assets are not expected to be consumed or sold in less than a year, and they therefore are categorized as Long Term Assets.

Fixed assets are tangible: you can see them, touch them, and point them out. The common categories of fixed assets are:

- Equipment (office and plant equipment)
- Furniture & Fixtures
- Vehicles
- Buildings
- Leasehold Improvements (for improvements you make to real estate you're renting)

You should create Fixed Asset accounts for each category of fixed assets that are applicable to your business (almost all businesses track Equipment and Furniture & Fixtures, the other categories may not apply to your business).

What is Depreciation?

The Internal Revenue Service Publication 946 offers the following definition of depreciation: "An annual income tax deduction that allows you to recover the cost or other basis of certain property over the time you use the property. It is an allowance for the wear and tear, deterioration, or obsolescence of the property." The IRS doesn't let you post the cost of a fixed asset as an expense.

Most fixed assets are depreciated, which means that some or all of the cost of the fixed asset each year is transferred to an expense account, which reduces your taxable profit for that year. Technically, the idea of depreciation is to depreciate the fixed asset so that the expense is recorded for each year that the fixed asset is expected to be useful. How long will a fixed asset last before breaking or becoming obsolete? If the answer is five years, logic tells us that the cost is recovered at the rate of 20% of the original cost each year for five years.

Of course, it isn't that simple. Some fixed assets are hard to define in terms of deterioration or obsolescence (I've never met anyone who could define, with absolute certainty, the useful life of a computer or of the shelves in a warehouse).

In addition, the Internal Revenue Service has devised a complicated set of rules and methods for taking depreciation for certain types fixed assets.

Depreciation amounts should be computed by your accountant, who normally uses the IRS allowed amounts. When you have those numbers you enter the depreciation expense and reduce the current value of the fixed asset in your books. This is usually done annually as part of tax preparation. The steps involved in this task are discussed in Chapter 10.

Purchasing a Fixed Asset

Depending on the type of asset, most businesses purchase a fixed asset in one of the following ways:

- Pay cash (write a check).
- Obtain a loan (or mortgage).

It's also common to combine these methods, using cash for a down payment and financing the rest.

NOTE: The cost of a fixed asset includes everything involved with buying it; this includes shipping, sales tax, and any other fees or costs added to the purchase price.

Because tracking fixed assets and their depreciation is a time consuming task (and you're paying your accountant to perform the task), you and your accountant need to agree upon a minimum amount for posting equipment, fixtures, furniture, etc. as a fixed asset.

For example, if you buy a new computer monitor, or a new router for your network, the cost is quite low compared to the cost of buying a major fixed asset. If you and your accountant have agreed on a $250.00 minimum threshold for treating a purchase as a fixed asset, purchases below $250.00 are posted to an expense account. You can create an expense account named Office Expenses, or Equipment Accessories, or something similar and use that account to record the purchase as an expense.

Cash Purchase of a Fixed Asset

Most cash purchases of fixed assets are for the Equipment and Furniture & Fixtures categories (because the other fixed asset categories are usually for things too expensive to purchase without financing). When you write a check or post a credit card payment for something that qualifies as a fixed asset, post the payment to the appropriate fixed asset account. This creates a transaction journal that resembles Table 5-14.

Account	Debit	Credit
1501 – Equipment	500.00	
1000 – Bank Account		500.00

Table 5-14: Fixed asset purchases are posted to the appropriate fixed asset account.

Financed Purchase of a Fixed Asset

If you're financing a fixed asset you have to track the value of the asset and you also have to track the loan. For the portion of the cost that's financed, no bank account is involved because you didn't expend funds.

The loan is a liability to your business, and the easiest way to track both the asset and the loan is to create a journal entry that resembles the transaction seen in Table 5-15.

Account	Debit	Credit
1501 – Equipment	5000.00	
2300 – Bank Loan #1234		5000.00

Table 5-15: This asset comes with a bank loan; both the asset and the loan need to be entered in your books.

If you used a check or credit card for the down payment, the amount was posted to the fixed asset. When you create the journal entry for the loan, the amount of the loan is also posted to the fixed asset. Now, the total cost of the fixed asset appears in the fixed asset account. Tracking loan payments (including interest and principal) is covered in Chapter 6.

Intangible Assets

Unlike a fixed asset (which is something you can see), an intangible asset is one that doesn't exist as a physical entity – it's not "fixed" the way furniture and equipment can be fixed in the workplace.

However, an intangible asset has value because, like any asset, it is something that belongs to your company. Usually, an intangible asset is unique to your company.

Depending on the intangible asset and the manner in which it was acquired, you might be able to amortize the asset, which means you can create an expense that reduces your net profit (and therefore reduces your tax burden).

Intellectual Property

For small businesses, the common intangible assets are patents, copyrights, and trademarks (called *intellectual property*).

Payments for intellectual property are normally paid by check against amounts invoiced by a vendor. In many cases, the total cost of the property is billed in sequential amounts over time (for example, a deposit to an attorney to begin the process and then progress payments until the process is completed). These partial payments are accumulated in a *deposit account* (a Current Asset) until the asset is fully acquired, as seen in Table 5-16.

Account	Debit	Credit
1302 – Deposits on Patent	2000.00	
1000 – Bank Account		2000.00

Table 5-16: Track payments made to acquire intellectual property in an Asset deposit account.

When the asset is fully acquired, create a journal entry to reclassify the funds posted to the Deposit asset into an intangible asset, as seen in Table 5-17.

Account	Debit	Credit
1801 – Patent	7000.00	
1302 – Deposits on Patent		7000.00

Table 5-17: Reclassify the progress payments when the asset is fully acquired.

Organizational Costs

Organizational costs are the expenses you incurred to form and begin your business. This could include legal fees, incorporation charges, fictitious name registration charges, and other pre-operating costs.

Often these costs are advanced by business owners before the business bank accounts are set up. In this case, create a journal entry to reflect money owed to the owner by the business for the payments (which is a liability to the business), as seen in Table 5-18.

Account	Debit	Credit
1901 – Organizational Costs	2500.00	
2301 – Advances due to Owner		2500.00

Table 5-18: Record organizational costs that will be repaid to the owner as a liability.

If the advances are considered capital contributions from the owner, the credits are made to the applicable capital accounts (depending on the type of entity) instead of the advance account. Discuss this decision with your accountant. Chapter 7 covers owner contributions and capital accounts.

(If the payments for organizational costs are made directly from the business bank account, post the checks directly to the Organizational Costs asset.)

Goodwill

Goodwill is the premium paid to acquire business assets in excess of their fair value. The Goodwill asset is usually created when a new owner acquires an existing business. The amount is normally agreed upon between the buyer and seller along with the value of the other assets being purchased. Table 5-19 shows how the acquisition of an existing business is usually recorded.

Account	Debit	Credit
1301 – Inventory	2500.00	
1501 – Equipment	5000.00	
1950 – Goodwill	2500.00	
1000 – Bank Account		10000.00

Table 5-19: Record the cost of purchasing a company by specifying each component of the purchase price.

What is Amortization?

Amortization for intangible assets is similar to depreciation for fixed assets. The rules concerning asset life spans and expensing rates are listed in Internal Revenue Service Publication 535.

Like depreciation of fixed assets, the entries required to record the annual amortization expenses that reduce the book value of your intangible assets should be provided by your accountant. Chapter 10 has additional information concerning amortization expense.

Chapter 6

Managing Liabilities

A liability is something you owe to someone else. It is money or goods you may be holding, or have the use of, but those things don't belong to you. For example, goods or services you've received but haven't yet paid for are liabilities (Accounts Payable). Also, money you are holding for someone else and will pass along to its rightful owner is a liability (payroll withholding, sales tax you've collected). In this chapter I cover the common liabilities that small businesses encounter. (I cover payroll liabilities in Chapter 9.)

Accounts Payable

Your Accounts Payable (A/P) account represents the money you currently owe vendors for goods and services you purchased to run your business. A/P accumulates when you enter vendor bills into your accounting system. When you pay the bills (posted as *bill payments*), the A/P total decreases by the amount of the payments.

It isn't necessary to track A/P; instead, you can store vendor bills in a folder and then just write checks (called *direct disbursements* instead of *bill payments*). Direct disbursements work best if you always pay your bills in full, because there's no need to track money still owed to your vendors. Direct disbursements are covered in Chapter 4.

Entering Vendor Bills

When you enter a vendor bill into your books, the credit side of the transaction is posted to A/P. The debit side of the transaction is posted to the appropriate account(s) for the expense. The transaction is part of your Purchases Journal. Table 6-1 shows the purchases journal for a vendor bill that covers more than one expense. Many (if not most) bills cover a single expense, and you enter only that expense in the transaction.

Account	Debit	Credit
6060 – Office Supplies	105.50	
6800 – Shipping	10.10	
2100 – Accounts Payable		115.60

Table 6-1: The total expenses equal the amount posted to A/P.

In addition to creating the transaction that posts the totals to your general ledger, you must track the amounts owed to each vendor. If you're using accounting software, this is done automatically. However, if you're keeping books manually, or in Excel, you must create pages or columns for each vendor.

Periodically, you should run a report on A/P, which means you list all the vendors to whom you owe money. The total of the vendor A/P balances must match the total of the A/P account.

Paying Vendor Bills

When you pay a vendor bill that you've entered into your books, the bill payment credits (reduces) the bank account and debits (reduces) the A/P account, as seen in Table 6-2.

Account	Debit	Credit
1000 – Bank Account		115.60
2100 – Accounts Payable	115.60	

Table 6-2: Paying an existing vendor bill reduces A/P.

Many business owners look at the posting for the check that paid a bill and wonder why they don't see the expense accounts covered by the transaction. When you use A/P to enter bills and pay them, the postings for the bill payment have nothing to do with the expenses incurred; those expenses were posted when you entered the bill.

You need to think of this process as two transactions that are both linked to A/P; the first transaction records the expense and increases A/P, the second transaction reduces A/P and your bank account.

If you don't use A/P (you don't enter the vendor bills into your books), but instead you just write checks, those checks are posted directly to the expense accounts.

WARNING: Most accounting software has separate commands for writing checks (direct disbursements) and paying bills that were entered in the software. Be sure to choose the correct function.

If you make a partial payment, the unpaid balance remains on the vendor's record and is included in the total of the A/P account in the general ledger. As additional bills arrive the balance grows, and as you chip away at the balance with additional payments, the A/P reports track your progress.

You can, of course, make a vendor payment that covers multiple vendor bills; if so, be sure to keep a record of which bills are paid or partially paid (accounting software tracks this automatically). Tracking the vendor's bill number and date is important when you have to have a conversation with the vendor about your account.

Customer Upfront Deposits

If a customer gives you a deposit against a sale, the prepayment isn't income to you because you haven't earned it by delivering the goods or services. The money belongs to the customer until you earn it. Usually, customer deposits are requested for products that are custom made, or for new customers who have ordered expensive goods or services. Because it's not your money (yet), a deposit is a liability. The liability is removed when you earn the money and present the customer with an invoice.

To track customer deposits, you must create a Current Liability account named Customer Deposits. In addition, you must set up the customer record to track these deposits, so you know how much to deduct when you create the final invoice.

The amount of money posted to Customer Deposits represents the amount of your bank account balance you can't spend. It's not your money yet. If you take many customer deposits, you should open a separate bank account to track and segregate these amounts. As you apply the prepayment to the customer's final invoice, the money becomes yours and you can transfer it to your regular bank account.

Recording a Customer Deposit

Customer deposits usually arrive in one of two ways: A conversation in which you ask the customer to send a deposit, or an invoice you send to request the deposit.

If there is no invoice, the income is posted to the Customer Deposits liability account when you deposit the funds, as seen in Table 6-3.

Account	Debit	Credit
1000 – Bank Account	200.00	
2800 – Customer Deposits		200.00

Table 6-3: Deposit a customer's prepayment as a liability, not as income.

If you create an invoice for the upfront deposit, post the invoice to the Customer Deposits liability account, to create the posting journal seen in Table 6-4.

Account	Debit	Credit
1100 – Accounts Receivable	200.00	
2800 – Customer Deposits		200.00

Table 6-4: An invoice increases both A/R and the Customer Deposits totals.

NOTE: A customer deposit is not taxable; the taxes are applied when you send an invoice for the sale.

When the customer pays the invoice, the posting for that transaction debits (increases) the bank account and credits (reduces) A/R

Applying a Customer Deposit to a Sale

When it's time to collect the money for the sale, you have to reduce the total amount of the invoice by the amount of the upfront deposit you received from the customer. However, you have to show the total amount of the sale, not the net amount collected, as income. Here's how to prepare the invoice:

1. Enter the full price of the sale (goods or services), which is posted to Income. If there are multiple

goods and/or services involved, enter each one at its full price.

2.   On the last line of the invoice, enter the amount of the deposit with a minus sign (to reduce the net amount of the invoice) and post that to the Customer Deposits account.

3.   If the sale is taxable, the sales tax is applied to the total amount of sold goods (the amount posted to income). The customer deposit has no effect on the amount of sales tax; it only affects the amount due from the customer.

The resulting posting journal correctly reduces the customer deposit account, and increases income and A/R. Table 6-5 displays the posting journal for a taxable (7%) sale of $1000.00 where the customer prepaid $200.00. If you don't collect sales tax, the amount due is merely the total sale less the customer deposit.

Account	Debit	Credit
4000 – Income		1000.00
2800 – Customer Deposits	200.00	
2100 – Sales Tax Payable		70.00
1100 – Accounts Receivable	870.00	

Table 6-5: The invoice takes the prepayment into consideration.

Client Retainers

Businesses that provide ongoing professional services (attorneys, accountants, financial advisors, technical support companies, and so on) frequently collect retainers against which they take their fees. The customer sends a certain amount of money that is held as a deposit against payment of future invoices. As you perform the work, your invoices "spend down" the retainer. When the retainer amount is too low to cover the next invoices, you collect another retainer from the customer.

If retainers are your normal method of doing business with clients, it's a good idea to open a separate bank account for them (a business savings account or money market provides interest). If you deposit the money into your regular business account, you have to track the total amount of retainers (which matches the total in the Retainers liability account) to make sure that amount is always available in the bank account.

> **NOTE**: Some professions, such as attorneys, are required to maintain separate bank accounts called escrow accounts for client funds. Escrow accounts are covered in the next section.

Receiving Retainers

To track retainers, you need a Current Liability account named Retainers. When a client sends a retainer, you post the bank deposit to that Retainers account, as seen in Table 6-6.

Account	Debit	Credit
1000 – Bank Account	2000.00	
2900 –Retainers Held		2000.00

Table 6-6: The posting journal for receiving retainer funds.

Remember that the total of the funds in the Retainers liability account represents the amount of money in the bank account that isn't yours to spend. If you maintain a separate bank account for retainers, it's easy to make sure the amounts in the two accounts always match. If you deposit retainers into your regular bank account you must mentally subtract the total in the Retainers liability account from the balance so you don't spend down into retainers when you issue checks to pay expenses.

Applying Retainers to Invoices

Money you received as a retainer becomes spendable when you earn it. At that point, the funds are changed from a liability to income. When you invoice your client for services performed, you transfer the retainer funds to income. Here's how to create an invoice for a client who has sent a retainer:

1. Enter the amount for services, and post that amount to Income.

2. Enter a line "Applied from Retainer", posted to the retainer liability account. Enter the amount with a minus sign to reduce the amount of the invoice.

If the retainer balance is larger than the invoice amount, only apply a retainer amount equal to the invoice amount. This creates a zero-amount invoice, but you've transferred these retainer funds into income and you can spend the money.

If the retainer balance is smaller than the invoice amount, apply the entire retainer balance to create an invoice for the net amount due from the client. Then issue a separate invoice for additional retainer funds.

As you can see, this system makes it very important to track retainer funds on a client-by-client basis.

- If you're using accounting software you can create reports on the postings to the retainer account, sorting the reports by client name.

- If you're keeping client records manually or in Excel, you must track each client's retainer account in a separate page or column.

The process of creating the invoice automatically turns the retainer funds into income by reducing the amount in the Retainers liability fund and increasing the amount posted to income. Table 6-7 represents a posting journal for a client who sent a $2000.00 retainer that is being used to pay an invoice in the amount of $1400.00.

Account	Debit	Credit
4000 – Income		1400.00
2900 – Retainers Held	1400.00	

Table 6-7: The retainers account is decreased and the income account is increased.

In this example, the client's bill is paid in full by retainer funds. Nothing posts to A/R because there's no balance due from the client. However, the Retainers account is decreased and that amount is moved into Income, because now you've earned the money. (It's time to issue another invoice for retainer funds.)

If you maintain a separate bank account for retainer funds, transfer the amount of the retainer that was entered on the invoice to your regular bank account. You can spend it now.

Tracking Escrow

Escrow funds (also called *trust funds*) are liabilities because they don't belong to you; they belong to your client. Managing escrow funds differs from managing retainers and customer deposits in two ways:

- The funds belong to your client, but are not collected from that client. Instead, they're collected from a third party on behalf of your client.

- The rules for managing escrow funds are mandated by state law and the rules of your professional association.

All states require attorneys to maintain a separate bank account for escrow funds, and to impose strict bookkeeping procedures for tracking escrow funds as liabilities. Professional associations impose similar rules on other professions, such as realtors, agents, and others who collect funds from third parties on behalf of clients.

To manage escrow you must open a separate bank account for escrow funds and add that bank account to your chart of accounts. Track each client's escrow carefully, so you always know the amount in the escrow fund for each client. (Or, you can open separate escrow bank accounts for each client).

You must also create a liability account for escrowed funds, usually named Funds Held In Trust. Because all transactions are linked to a client, your client records make it easy to track which funds in the liability account belong to which client. However, you may be more comfortable creating separate liability accounts for each client.

The total of the funds in the liability account (or the combined totals of multiple liability accounts) must always equal the total of the funds in the escrow bank account (or the combined total of all the escrow bank accounts).

Every transaction that involves an escrow bank account, whether it's money coming in or money going out, must follow these rules with absolutely no exceptions:

- The transaction must be posted to the Funds Held In Trust liability account.

- A client must be linked to the transaction.

Receiving Funds into an Escrow Bank Account

Money that is deposited into an escrow account comes from a third party for the benefit of a client. This is not income. You deposit the money by posting the transaction to the liability account you set up to track escrow funds, as seen in Table 6-8. You must also include the transaction in the client's record (software does this automatically, because you receive the money using the client as the customer).

Account	Debit	Credit
1050 – Escrow Bank Account	10000.00	
2600 – Funds Held in Trust		10000.00

Table 6-8: Escrow funds are always posted to the liability account that tracks escrow.

Disbursing Escrow Funds

Depending on your profession, a variety of payments may be due after funds have been deposited in an escrow account.

For example, real estate professionals track the buyer's down payment or "earnest money" (money accompanying the offer) as escrow when the buyer's offer is accepted. Usually, when the sale is complete (at settlement), the escrow funds are disbursed to the seller. If the sale falls through, the escrow money is disbursed in accordance with the terms of the contract that was signed by both the buyer and the seller (usually called the *Agreement of Sale*).

Attorneys usually have the most complicated set of disbursements from escrow, including repayments of costs paid in advance, internal costs incurred by the law firm, the legal fee due the law firm, and, of course, the client's proceeds.

Here are the guidelines for disbursing escrow funds:

- All checks are written from the escrow bank account.

- All checks are posted to the liability account for escrow.

- All checks are linked to and recorded in the client's record.

Most attorneys create separate checks for reimbursed expenses, internal expenses, and the firm's fee. The payee is the same; this is just a way to create an audit trail. The IRS advises that hard costs (real outlays for expenses) and soft costs (internal/overhead costs) should be tracked separately.

Sales & Use Tax

If the goods or services you sell are taxable in your state (or in any state in which you have an office or warehouse), you must collect sales tax from your customers and remit the money to the state tax authorities.

Use tax applies when you buy something that is taxable in your state without paying sales tax, usually because the vendor is in another state. (Use tax applies in other scenarios too, and they are covered in this section.)

Tracking Sales Tax

Sales tax is not income or expense, it's a liability. You're holding someone else's money (sent by your customer; but belonging to the state and/or local tax authorities), and you pass it along to the tax authorities.

Sales tax is added to the sales you generate when both the customer and the goods/services you're selling are taxable. That means that sometimes taxable goods or services aren't taxed, because the customer isn't taxable. And, sometimes a taxable customer isn't charged sales tax because the particular goods or services you sold that customer aren't taxable.

NOTE: Chapter 3 has details on defining and tracking taxable customers, goods, and services, as well as posting the sales tax when you generate a sale.

Of course, the easiest way to deal with sales tax would be to track sales tax by posting it to a liability account named Sales Tax Payable every time a sale involves sales tax, and then sending a check for the total amount in the liability account to the state.

Unfortunately, it doesn't usually work that way. Most states want reports that include a lot more information than "how much tax did you collect?" including (but not necessarily limited to):

- Total sales for the reporting period.

- Total taxable sales for the reporting period for the state sales tax.

- Total nontaxable sales for the reporting period for the state sales tax.

- Total taxable sales for the reporting period for additional local sales taxes.

- Total nontaxable sales for the reporting period for additional local sales taxes.

- Total sales tax collected for the reporting period for the state sales tax.

- Total sales tax collected for the reporting period for additional local sales tax.

In some states, there's a separate form for each local sales tax, as well as a different vendor name and address for sending the reports and money. Some states have special sales tax rates for specific goods or services and those amounts are reported separately.

You need to make sure you enter all your sales transactions in a way that makes the data that's required available. Check the forms for your state (most states only accept sales tax reports and remittances online). Then, make sure you can easily ascertain the totals required for your report. (If you're using accounting software, the Sales Tax feature should produce the totals you need.)

Work with your accountant to make sure you're accumulating the financial information you need to report and remit sales tax for the states in which you hold a sales tax license.

Tracking Use Tax

Use tax is an amount due to your state sales tax authority to make up for lost sales tax revenue when you purchase or use something that's taxable without remitting sales tax to your vendor at the time of your purchase.

Most states that have sales tax laws also have use tax laws. The laws apply to everyone; consumers and all businesses (even businesses that don't have a sales tax license because they don't provide taxable goods or services). Everyone is expected to send a use tax payment whenever they purchase an item that would be taxable in the state of residence, but the purchase did not include the payment of sales tax (usually because it was purchased from a vendor in another state or over the Internet).

Collecting use tax from every household in the state and from businesses that don't have a sales tax license is an overwhelming task. It's easier for state revenue departments to go after businesses that have a sales tax license, and that's exactly what most states are doing. States describe this as an "easy-to-find" group; some business owners call it the "sitting duck" group.

Each state that imposes sales taxes defines the conditions under which use tax is due. In most states, the following scenarios make you liable for use tax:

- You purchased goods or services that are taxable in your state from an out-of-state vendor, and paid no tax.

- You purchased goods or services that are taxable in your state from an out-of-state vendor, but paid that vendor sales tax at a rate lower than your home state's rate.

- You purchased taxable items for resale (inventory) without paying sales tax (because you have a sales tax license), but you used an item in your business instead of selling it.

Unlike sales tax, which is money you collect from customers and turn over to the state (making it neither income nor expense), use tax is a business expense.

Tracking Use Tax for Purchases

The most efficient way to track use tax is to record it when the underlying purchase transaction that created the use tax liability is recorded. In addition to recording the expense, the check you write (or the vendor bill you enter in your books) posts the use tax due (a liability) and the use tax expense (an expense).

Use the following steps to enter a bill or write a direct check to a vendor for which use tax is due:

1. Enter the expense account for the purchase you made (which matches the total amount of the transaction).

2. Enter the Use Tax expense account for the use tax amount due to your state.

3. Enter the Use tax expense amount with a minus, and post to the Use Tax Due liability account you've set up.

Because the last two items wash each other out (they are for the same amount but one is a negative number), it doesn't change the amount of the money being sent to the vendor.

Table 6-9 represents the posting journal for a payment of $200.00 made by a Pennsylvania company to an out-of-state vendor who didn't charge sales tax (Pennsylvania has a 6 % sales tax)

Account	Debit	Credit
6200 – Computer Supplies	200.00	
2120 – Use Tax Payable		12.00
7110 – Use Tax Expense	12.00	
1000 – Bank Account		200.00

Table 6-9: Tracking use tax doesn't change the amount of the purchase.

If the transaction you're creating is a vendor bill instead of a check, the A/P account receives the posting instead of the bank account. When you pay the vendor's bill the bank account and the A/P account balances are reduced.

When you remit the Use Tax to the state, post the payment to the Use Tax Due liability account to wash the balance accumulated in the liability account. The amount you posted to Use Tax Expense stays on the books.

Depending on the reporting requirements for your state, you may need to adopt a different procedure to track the use tax you owe on purchases. Confer with your accountant to make sure you keep records that match the way your state collects information.

Tracking Use Tax for Items You Use in Your Business

If you remove inventory normally held for sale from your warehouse for your own business use, you owe use tax on the removed item. After all, if you'd sold the inventory to a customer, tax would have been added to the sale and the state would have received its money.

Luckily, most states impose the use tax for withdrawn inventory items based on the cost of the item, not the retail price. Be sure to check the law in your state before assuming you can create the transaction based on cost.

If you use accounting software that includes inventory tracking, you have an inventory adjustment feature built in. The feature automatically changes the Quantity on Hand and applies the current cost of the item to the transaction, crediting (reducing) the value of the inventory asset account and debiting (increasing) the offset account you select in the transaction window.

Use the following steps to remove inventory and then create the use tax transaction:

1. In the software's Inventory Adjustment transaction window, reduce the quantity of the item and select Office Expenses as the offsetting account. Save the transaction and close the transaction window.

2. Then create a journal entry that debits Use Tax Expense and credits the Use Tax owed liability account. When you remit the use tax to the state, the payment is posted to the Use Tax owed liability account (washing the original posting in your journal entry); the expense remains on the books.

If you don't use accounting software, create a journal entry to post all the components involved in the transaction. Use the information in Table 6-10 (which assumes an item cost of $100.00 in a state that has a 6 % use tax) as a guideline.

Account	Debit	Credit
1100 – Inventory Asset		100.00
6510 – Office Supplies	100.00	
7110 – Use Tax Expense	6.00	
2120 – Use Tax Payable		6.00

Table 6-10: Track inventory value and use tax in a single journal entry.

Don't forget to adjust the Quantity on Hand of the item in your inventory records.

Tracking Use Tax for Other Uses of Taxable Items

There are other scenarios in which you take inventory out of stock. For example, two common reasons for removing inventory are to make a donation of the inventory item to a nonprofit organization, or to send a sample or premium to a customer.

In many states, either of those actions triggers a requirement to remit use tax. Use the instructions and guidelines in the previous section to track the use tax, except when you offset the inventory reduction use either the Charitable Contributions expense account or the Advertising and Marketing expense account in place of the previous example's Office Supplies expense.

Loans to Your Company

Many businesses occasionally need loans to operate. Common reasons for loans include a vehicle purchase, a real estate purchase, expansion of inventory and/or staff, etc. You need to track the loan and your payments in your accounting books.

Current Liabilities Vs. Long Term Liabilities

The standard definition of a current liability is that the debt is expected to be paid within a year. Accounts Payable, payroll withholdings, sales tax payable, and other similar debts are current liabilities.

Liabilities that are expected to be paid off over a period longer than a year are usually classified as long-term liabilities.

The reason to track current liabilities separately from long term liabilities is that lenders, potential investors, financial analysts, and business owners frequently want to see separate totals for the two types of liabilities. They usually compare the current liabilities to the current assets (which include cash, A/R, Inventory, and any other asset that is expected to turn into cash within a year.) These figures provide a quick way to determine the current health of a business.

These definitions aren't etched in stone, so check with your accountant to determine the type of liability account you should create for each loan.

Entering a Loan

To track a loan you need to set up a liability account. Most loans are classified as Long Term Liabilities, but your accountant may want to set up a short-term loan as a current liability.

If you received the proceeds of the loan in the form of a check or a direct deposit into your bank account, create a cash receipt transaction that posts the bank deposit to the liability account for the loan. Table 6-11 represents the deposit of loan proceeds.

Account	Debit	Credit
1000 –Bank Account	10000.00	
2220 – Loan #887453		10000.00

Table 6-11: The money deposited into the bank is posted to the loan liability account.

Sometimes the loan doesn't result in a check; instead the loan covers the purchase of an asset. In this case, create a journal entry to track both the asset and the loan, as seen in Table 6-12.

Account	Debit	Credit
1510 – Fixed Asset-Vehicle	20000.00	
2220 – Loan #887453		20000.00

Table 6-12: This loan covers the purchase of an asset without the receipt of cash.

Often, a loan for a fixed asset or another large purchase is accompanied by a down payment. The down payment is also posted to the fixed asset to make sure the total cost of the asset is recorded. Check with your accountant to see how he or she wants you to create multiple transactions for the new asset.

Making Loan Payments

Loans are liabilities, but the interest you pay is a deductible business expense. As you make loan payments you need to separate the amount applied to principal from the amount applied to interest.

Some loans have fixed amounts for principal and interest on the outstanding balance each month; other loans are set up to pay a constant amount that is less interest and more principal with each payment. For the latter, you need to get an amortization schedule from the lender so you know how to split each payment.

Whether you write a check or have your loan payment automatically deducted from your bank account, here are the guidelines for creating the payment:

- The amount of the payment is the total amount due to the lender (both principal and interest).

- The total amount of the payment is split between two posting accounts; post the principal to the loan's liability account and the interest to your interest expense account.

If you can't determine the amount of the principal and interest, post the entire payment to the loan's liability account. When the lender sends you a statement of interest, your accountant can instruct you on the steps to take to journalize the interest to an expense. Be sure the journal entry is dated in the appropriate year.

Line of Credit

A line of credit is like a loan that you can use if and when the need arises. The advantage of a line of credit over a loan is that interest is charged only on the amount of the line of credit that you have drawn from the total amount available. A line of credit is issued with a maximum amount, but you only need to track the amount you've drawn and is therefore outstanding.

There are a variety of plans that financial institutions use to award and track a line of credit, but for this discussion I'll assume your line of credit follows the common scenario:

- When you need to draw on the line of credit, the financial institution transfers the amount you request into your bank account.

- The financial institution collects interest on the amount currently drawn. (Frequently the interest is automatically deducted from your bank account).

- There are no regularly scheduled payments for repaying principal.

Entering a Draw on Your Line of Credit

You need to create a liability account for your line of credit. Most of the time, a line of credit is categorized as a long-term liability, but the terms of your agreement with the financial institution, and the maximum amount available, may permit your accountant to suggest a current liability account.

Every time you draw on the line of credit, the transaction is a deposit to your bank account that is posted to the line of credit liability account, as seen in Table 6-13.

Account	Debit	Credit
1000 –Bank Account	3000.00	
2230 – Line of Credit #55567		3000.00

Table 6-13: When you draw on a line of credit, your bank account and your liability are increased.

As you write checks from your bank account to pay expenses, the payments have nothing to do with the line of credit. You post the transactions normally, ignoring the fact that the money came from a line of credit.

Paying Interest on a Line of Credit

The interest on your line of credit is based on the amount you've drawn. If you write a check for interest to the financial institution, post the check to your Interest expense account. If the money is automatically withdrawn from your bank account, create a "fake" check, which is a check with no number or with the text EFT (electronic funds transfer) used as the number.

Either way, the transaction journal shows the same posting. As you can see in Table 6-14, interest payments don't post to the liability account you created to track the line of credit.

Account	Debit	Credit
1000 –Bank Account		110.00
6200 – Interest Expense	110.00	

Table 6-14: Interest paid on the funds drawn from a line of credit is posted just like any other interest payment.

Repaying Line of Credit Principal

When you want to reduce your interest expense, you pay down your line of credit to reduce the balance. Your payment is posted to the liability account, as seen in Table 6-15.

Account	Debit	Credit
1000 –Bank Account		2800.00
2230 – Line of Credit #55567	2800.00	

Table 6-15: Post principal payments to the liability account for the line of credit

Of course, future interest payments are based on the remaining balance in the liability account.

Chapter 7

Managing Equity

I'm assuming you consulted an attorney and an accountant to decide how to set up your business. In this chapter I explain how to post transactions related to the money you put into your business and the money you take out of the business. I'll discuss the following types of entities.

- **Proprietorship**. A business owned by a single individual.

- **Partnership**. A business owned by more than one individual.

- **LLC (Limited Liability Company)**. A business that has one or more owners (called *members* instead of owners). Note that the "C" in LLC stands for company, not corporation. A single member LLC is similar to a proprietorship and a multimember LLC is similar to a partnership. An LLC provides more protection against personal liability than a proprietorship or a partnership. An LLC can request permission of the IRS to be treated as a corporation; if granted, the discussions in this chapter follow the rules of C Corporations.

- **LLP (Limited Liability Partnership)**. Similar to a partnership but providing more protection against personal liability. Each partner is called a *member* instead of partner.

- **S Corporation**. A hybrid organization with some characteristics of a proprietorship or partnership, and some characteristics of a C Corporation.

- **C Corporation**. The entity type most controlled by rules, including the way the stockholder (owner) funds the corporation and withdraws funds.

For all of these entities the discussions in this chapter involve the use of equity accounts in transactions that withdraw money from your business. Some of these transactions segregate information you use in preparing income tax returns. Income tax discussions, while mentioned in this chapter, are discussed in further detail in Chapter 10.

Understanding Equity Accounts

Equity is your business' capital, the difference between what it owns (assets) and what it owes (liabilities). Equity is increased by the money owners put into the business (startup funds, additional funds for growth) and by the company's profit. Equity is decreased by business losses and by withdrawals (not including payroll) made by the business owners.

WARNING: For income tax purposes, owners are taxed on the profit and loss of the business, not the amount of funds they withdraw.

The equity accounts are the best reminder of an important concept that some business owners don't understand: Not all of your bank deposits are income, not all of your checks are expenses. Transactions that involve equity accounts are neither income nor expenses; these transactions don't affect the taxable profit/loss of the company.

The simplified definition of "equity" is "what the owner's stake in the company is worth". The owner can be a proprietor, a partner, a member, or a stockholder. Equity transactions appear on the Balance Sheet report, not on the Profit & Loss report, because the Profit & Loss report is only concerned with income and expenses. (Details about those reports and what they represent are in Chapter 11.)

There are a variety of equity accounts you use when you post equity-based transactions, and it's important to understand how and when to use each equity account. Equity accounts track the net effect of all of your company's past transactions and are the starting point in calculating the value of your business.

Using these accounts correctly also means you won't have a hassle with the IRS because you incorrectly reported an equity transaction as an expense, or because you failed to report the correct amount of personal income from the business on your personal tax return.

Proprietorships

A proprietorship (also called a *sole proprietorship*) has a single owner, and doesn't file a business tax return. Instead, the profit for the business is reported on Schedule C of the owner's federal tax return and is included on the owner's personal income tax return (Form 1040). There is no limit to the number of proprietorships that can be included on an individual tax return. Each proprietorship requires its own Schedule C (based on each individual company's profit and loss report), and the amount reported on Form 1040 is the sum of all Schedule Cs included with the tax return.

It's best to run your proprietorship with a separate bank account dedicated to your business operations. Although this isn't strictly required, handling your business operations in this manner makes record keeping easier, and provides a record that a third party (tax authority, a bank considering loaning your business money, etc.) could examine without confusing your personal finances with your business activities.

Funding Proprietorships

When you started your business, you probably funded it by transferring money from your personal bank account to the business account. Those startup funds are not income to the business and don't result in any taxable profit. You record this startup transaction as seen in Table 7-1

Account	Debit	Credit
1000 – Bank Account	1000.00	
3100 – Owner Contributions		1000.00

Table 7-1: The initial contribution of capital to a proprietorship is posted to an equity account – it isn't income.

Occasionally you may find it necessary to add additional capital to the business in order to fund operations. The additional funding is recorded in exactly the same way.

Withdrawing Money From a Proprietorship

As your proprietorship makes money, you can withdraw funds. It's important to note that the proprietor cannot take payroll (although you can hire employees who are on the payroll).

When you withdraw money, you post the amount as a contra (negative) transaction to equity. It's best to create a separate equity account named Draw to track your withdrawals. That way, both your contributions and draws are easy to see. You record the transaction as seen in Table 7-2.

Account	Debit	Credit
3500 –Draw	100.00	
1000 –Bank Account		100.00

Table 7-2: Record your withdrawal by posting the check to an equity account named Draw.

If you take money out of the cash register instead of writing a check to yourself, post the transaction to the account that tracks the register instead of the bank account.

Personal Expenses Paid by a Proprietorship

Many proprietors pay certain categories of expenses from the business bank account, even though those expenses are not deductible by the business. (Some of those expenses end up as deductions on your personal tax return.). The most common expenses managed this way are:

- **Charitable contributions**. Charitable contributions made by a sole proprietorship are not deductible by the business, but are deductible by the proprietor as if made personally.

- **Health insurance premiums**. If your business contributes to health insurance premiums for you and for employees, the premium payment for your own health insurance is not a business deduction. Premium payments for employees are deductible.

- **Retirement plan contributions**. Payment of a proprietor's retirement plan contributions are not deductible by a business, although payments made for employees are a business deduction,

- **Taxes**. Many proprietors pay their taxes from the business bank account, even though these payments are not a business expense.

I suggest you set up a specific Draw account for each of these payment types, instead of posting the payments to a single Draw account (reserving the account named Draw for general withdrawal of funds). This makes it easier to accumulate the totals for personal tax deductible payments that are not deductible on the business' Schedule C when you're getting ready for tax time. When you use business funds to make these payments, the transaction journal should resemble Table 7-3.

Account	Debit	Credit
3550 – Draw for Health Insurance	250.00	
3560 – Draw for Taxes	800.00	
1000 –Bank Account		1050.00

Table 7-3: Post payments for amounts that are transferred to the owner's personal tax return to specific Draw accounts.

In addition to these transactions, it's common for proprietorships to have payments made by the business that include some personal expenses in addition to business expenses (such as a credit card payment). It's efficient to pay the credit card bill from the business checking account instead of sending one business check and one personal check to the vendor. However, you must post the personal expenses to the owner's Draw account.

NOTE: It's best to use one credit card for business and another credit card for personal use. This makes your accounting tasks easier. However, many proprietors don't follow this advice and I present these examples as a way to deal with reality.

For example, let's say you used your credit card for gasoline for company use ($75.00) and also for gasoline for your personal use ($30.00). In addition, you purchased office supplies for your business ($100.00) and bought something personal ($20.00). The credit card bill is in the amount of $225.00. When you pay the credit card bill it must be posted as seen in Table 7-4.

Account	Debit	Credit
5100 – Automobile Expense	75.00	
6200 – Office Supplies	100.00	
3500 – Draw	50.00	
1000 – Bank Account		225.00

Table 7-4: This is the way to record the payment of a credit card bill that includes both business and personal expenses.

Partnerships

A partnership is an entity that operates like a proprietorship, but has more than one owner. The funding and withdrawal methods used by a partnership are determined by the agreement of the partners. A partnership files its taxes using federal Form 1065 and provides each partner with a Schedule K-1 that the partner uses in preparing his/her personal tax return.

The recording of capital contributions, withdrawals, and payment of personal expenses is the same as explained for Proprietorships in the preceding section. You need to create a separate equity account for each partner in your chart of accounts so you can supply accurate financial information to each partner for that partner's personal tax return.

In some partnerships, the contributions, draws, and the allocation of profits that are transferred to each partner's personal tax return are not the same for each partner. For example, your business may have three partners with different percentages of ownership:

- Partner A has a 50% interest

- Partner B has a 30% interest

- Partner C has a 20% interest

NOTE: Usually, the capital contributions and draws match the percentage of ownership, but that's not a legal requirement. All partners might contribute the same amount of startup money, but their share of the company's profits (declared on their personal income tax returns) match the agreed upon percentages.

Funding Partnerships

When you record the initial contribution of each partner you use the partners' individual equity accounts in the transaction journal, as seen in Table 7-5.

Account	Debit	Credit
1100 – Bank Account	10000.00	
3101 – Capital Contributions, Partner A		5000.00
3102 – Capital Contributions, Partner B		3000.00
3103 – Capital Contributions, Partner C		2000.00

Table 7-5: Posting of capital contributions by partners.

As the partnership continues its operations, its may be necessary to add additional capital to the business to fund its continuing operations. The additional funding is recorded the same way.

Withdrawing Money From a Partnership

Withdrawals of cash by the partners may be spelled out in the partnership agreement or the partners may instead periodically agree on the method of withdrawing money. As with a proprietorship, draw is not an expense; instead, it's an equity transaction. Draws are recorded as shown in Table 7-6.

Account	Debit	Credit
3501 –Draw Partner A	500.00	
3502 –Draw Partner B	300.00	
3503 –Draw Partner C	200.00	
1000 – Bank Account		1000.00

Table 7-6: Distribution of cash to partners is tracked in individual Draw accounts.

Just like proprietorships, there are several categories of expenses that businesses commonly pay out of their operating accounts that are not deductible by the partnership. Table 7-7 illustrates the way health insurance premiums paid for partners are recorded (health insurance paid for non-owner employees is a deductible business expense.). The transactions are for the actual premiums paid for each partner and may not be in proportion to their ownership interest.

The same format applies to using the business checking account to remit retirement plan contributions and personal taxes (both federal and state) on behalf of each partner.

Account	Debit	Credit
3551 – Draw Partner A Health Insurance Premiums	500.00	
3552 – Draw Partner B Health Insurance Premiums	500.00	
3553 – Draw Partner C Health Insurance Premiums	250.00	
1000 – Bank Account		1250.00

Table 7-7: Premium payments for partners' personal health insurance coverage are posted to each partner's equity account.

Paying Personal Expenses for Partners

As with a proprietorship, you may make payments of personal expenses on behalf of a partner to avoid sending multiple checks to the same vendor (such as a credit card payment that includes business and personal expenses). The personal expenses are posted to the appropriate partner's draw account, not to an expense account.

It's best to use one credit card for business and have each partner use a personal credit card for personal purchases. This makes your accounting tasks easier. However, many partnerships send business checks to vendors for amounts that include both business and personal expenses. Note that maintaining this paradigm can produce partnership balances that aren't in proportion to individual partner interests.

LLCs and LLPs

LLCs and LLPs provide more protection against personal liability than a proprietorship or a partnership. Owners are called members.

An LLC (Limited Liability Company) may be organized in either of the following ways:

- A single member LLC, which is similar to a proprietorship

- A multi-member LLC, which is similar to a partnership

An LLP (Limited Liability Partnership) provides more protection against personal liability than a standard partnership. It is similar to a multi-member LLC and is frequently used by professional businesses (for example, accountants, attorneys, architects, engineers, etc.) due to state regulations that will not permit them to form the business as an LLC.

Single Member LLC

A single member LLC has only one owner, called a *member*. For federal income tax purposes it is considered a disregarded entity (as if it does not exist) and is treated exactly the same as a proprietorship (discussed earlier in this chapter). The member files a Schedule C with his/her personal income tax return.

NOTE: While it is possible to request permission of the IRS to operate an LLC or an LLP as a corporation, it's unusual for a small business to do this.

Funding a Single Member LLC

Usually, a single member LLC is funded by transferring money from your personal bank account to the business account. Your investment of these funds is not income to the business and does not result in any taxable profit. It is recorded by increasing your bank balance and the member contribution balance as shown in Table 7-8.

Account	Debit	Credit
1000 – Bank Account	1000.00	
3100 – Member's Capital Contributions		1000.00

Table 7-8: Posting for the initial contribution of capital to a single member LLC.

As the business continues its operations, you may find it necessary to add additional capital to the business to fund its continuing operations. The additional funding is recorded in exactly the same way as the initial capital contribution.

Withdrawing Funds From a Single Member LLC

The net profit is available for withdrawal by the member. (As with a proprietorship, a single member LLC owner cannot take payroll.) The withdrawals are recorded by increasing an account named Draw, which is a contra (negative) equity account and is recorded as seen in Table 7-9.

Account	Debit	Credit
3500 – Member Draw	100.00	
1000 – Bank Account		100.00

Table 7-9: Withdrawal of profits by the member.

If you take money out of the cash register instead of writing a check to yourself, post the transaction to the account that tracks the register instead of the bank account.

It's common for a single member LLC to pay several categories of expenses from the business bank account that are not deductible by the business. Usually, these expenses are health insurance premiums, pension contributions, and payment of estimated income tax. As discussed earlier in this chapter for proprietorships, you should set up separate Draw accounts for each of these payments so you can easily see the totals when you're preparing your personal tax return.

Multimember LLCs and LLPs

The finances of multimember LLCs and LLPs are managed the same as partnerships (discussed earlier in this chapter). The only difference is that the owners of an LLP or a multimember LLC are called *members* instead of *partners*. Both of these entities file partnership tax returns (Form 1065) and provide each member with a Schedule K-1 that he/she uses in the preparation of personal income tax returns.

The funding and withdrawal methods used by an LLC are determined by the agreement of the members. The recording of capital contributions, withdrawals, payment of business expenses not deductible specifically by the business and the payment of personal expenses is the same as explained above with respect to partnerships except that the word "member" would be used in place of the word "partner" in the chart of accounts.

Funding Multimember LLCs and LLPs

The initial funding of an LLP or multimember LLC is usually accomplished by having the members deposit money into the business bank account. (Assets other than cash could also be contributed and their value needs to be acceptable to tax authorities and agreeable to the members.)

Initial contributions of cash or other assets are outlined in the organization agreement, and need not be equal among the members. These funds are not income; instead they are capital (equity). You post the transaction of startup capital as seen in Table 7-10.

Account	Debit	Credit
1100 – Bank Account	10000.00	
3101 – Member A Contribution		5000.00
3102 – Member B Contribution		3000.00
3103 – Member C Contribution		2000.00

Table 7-10: Posting contributions of members of an
LLP or multimember LLC.

You use the same method to add additional capital to the
business to fund its continuing operations.

Withdrawing Funds in Multimember LLCs and LLPs

Withdrawals of profits by members should be spelled out in the
organization agreement, or by periodic agreement of the partners.
These distributions are not an expense to the business; instead
they are withdrawals of equity. Table 7-11 displays the posting of
withdrawal of equity funds by members.

Account	Debit	Credit
3501 – Member A Distribution	500.00	
3502 – Member B Distribution	300.00	
3503 – Member C Distribution	200.00	
1000 – Bank Account		1000.00

Table 7-11: Distribution of funds to members of a LLP
or multimember LLC.

As with partnerships, several types of expenses (health
insurance, retirement plan payments, and income taxes) paid for
the members of multimember LLCs and LLPs are not deductible
by the business. Separate distribution accounts should be set up

for each member so that the information can be easily tracked for reporting the amounts to each member on the Schedule K-1 he/she receives at the end of the year.

Guaranteed Payments for Multimember LLCs and LLPs

Members of an LLC and LLP do not take salary. In some multimember LLCs and LLPs, there are some members who are active in the business and other members who are just passive investors. For the "working members", you can use a *guaranteed payment* to substitute for a salary. A guaranteed payment differs from payroll and draw (withdrawal of profits) in the following ways:

- Unlike payroll, no taxes are withheld from the payment. Instead, all applicable federal, state, and local taxes are paid by the individual members when they file their personal tax returns.

- Unlike a draw, a guaranteed payment is a tax deductible expense to the company. You need to set up an expense account to post the guaranteed payment.

TIP: Tax reporting requires that each member's guaranteed payments be reported individually, so I suggest setting up a separate guaranteed payment expense account for each member in your chart of accounts.

A guaranteed payment is recorded as shown in Table 7-12. Note that there is no guaranteed payment to Member B, who is a passive investor.

Account	Debit	Credit
6501 – Guaranteed Payments, Member A	4000.00	
6502 – Guaranteed Payments, Member C	2000.00	
1000 –Bank Account		6000.00

Table 7-12: Posting of guaranteed payments paid to members actively working in the company.

Many multimember LLCs and LLPs issue guaranteed payments to members when they issue payroll checks to employees. Since guaranteed payments are a substitute for payroll for working members, this makes sense.

If you do your payroll in-house, create the guaranteed payment checks the same day (but not through the payroll module since these payments have no payroll taxes withheld and are not included on your payroll reporting forms to the various tax authorities).

If you outsource your payroll you can ask the payroll service to issue the guaranteed payment checks. Make sure the payroll service sets up the members as a separate unit/department so that reports from the payroll service clearly show the deductions for employees and the lack of deductions for the members.

Guaranteed payments are not the same as a distribution of profits to members. The company's profit is reduced by the amount of the guaranteed payments because the guaranteed payments are considered direct expenses for the company.

The guaranteed payments are provided to each member on the Schedule K-1 he/she receives for income tax preparation at the end of the year. Members who receive guaranteed payments report both the guaranteed payments and their share of the profits on Schedule E of their personal tax returns (Form 1040).

Corporations

Corporations are the most formal form that an organization can choose. Part of the legal formation of a corporation is the issuance of stock (other parts include filing registrations in the business' home state and any other states in which the company does business). The number of authorized shares of stock is stated in the papers prepared by your attorney, as is the value of each share (called the *par value*).

Funding Corporations

To fund the corporation's startup, the corporation's founders purchase stock, usually purchasing only a portion of the authorized number of shares (to reserve some shares for future issue). Usually, the corporation's founders provide startup funds in an amount larger than the par value of the stock they purchase. The amount contributed over the par value for their stock is called *paid in capital*.

Table 7-13 shows the way the startup funding is posted for a corporation that issued 1000 shares of stock to the founders with a par value of $1.00 per share. A total of $10,000.00 was provided for startup, so $9000.00 in paid in capital is received. Both the stock purchases and the additional paid in capital are posted to Equity accounts.

Account	Debit	Credit
1000 –Bank Account	10000.00	
3100 – Stock		1000.00
3500 – Paid In Capital		9000.00

Table 7-13: Funding a corporation can be accomplished through stock purchases and additional capital contributed.

If the corporation requires additional funding to operate, additional stock can be issued, additional paid in capital can be received, or the corporation can borrow money.

Loans From Stockholders

It's common for stockholders to provide loans to the corporation, but you must work closely with your attorney if a stockholder loans funds to the company (there are strict rules about the way the loan must be documented and the amount of interest attached to the loan).

Loans are liabilities (amounts owed by the corporation) and the loan amount is not income. Table 7-14 displays the way a stockholder loan is posted.

Account	Debit	Credit
1100 –Bank Account	25000.00	
2520 – Loan Payable – Stockholder A		25000.00

Table 7-14: Create a liability account to track a loan from a stockholder.

C Corporations

C Corporations are the most formal types of business organizations. Some of the rules concerning financial transactions that affect stockholders are different from the rules for S Corporations (covered in the next section), and I go over the important financial transactions for C Corporations in this section.

C Corporation Stockholder Compensation

An active stockholder in the business is considered an employee of the corporation and his/her compensation (including both salary and benefits) is treated the same as for any other employee of the corporation. Salary for the stockholder/employee must be considered reasonable (neither too high nor too low) as loosely defined by the federal tax regulations; no attempt at a discussion of reasonableness is made in this book. (Chapter 9 covers payroll.)

A corporation can also pay directors' fees to active owners serving on its Board of Directors in compensation for their oversight of the business. These payments are usually tied to attendance at Board meetings. They are paid as subcontractor fees and are recorded as a charge to an account named Director Fee Expense. The expense is tax deductible by the corporation. The payments are reported on Form 1099, which is sent to the recipient. (Chapter 9 covers 1099 expenses.) Directors' fees are recorded as shown in Table 7-15.

Account	Debit	Credit
7200 – Directors' Fee Expense	1000.00	
1000 – Bank Account		1000.00

Table 7-15: Payment of director fees for attendance at a Board of Directors meeting.

C Corporation Profit Distributions

Dividend payments to stockholders, while not used by many corporations, are another way for the stockholders to take profit out of the business. The rules covering dividend payments are complicated, involving classes of stock, and you need to discuss this option and the way you post these transactions with your accountant.

Dividends are a reduction in equity and are a distribution of net income that was previously taxed to the C Corporation. Dividend payments are not expenses of the corporation, do not appear on the Profit & Loss report, and do not affect the net profit of the C Corporation.

C Corporation Taxation

A C Corporation is a taxable entity. It files and pays income taxes based on its profit and loss report using Form 1120.

S Corporations

An S Corporation can have either a single owner (stockholder) or multiple owners. An S Corporation must allocate all income and expense items in proportion to a stockholder's percentage ownership in the business' outstanding stock.

To take advantage of avoiding income taxes at the corporate level, consult with your attorney to be certain that forms have been filed with the appropriate tax authorities so the business is considered an S Corporation by the tax authorities. These forms are normally prepared in conjunction with the other incorporation papers for the business.

S Corporation Stockholder Compensation

An active stockholder in an S corporation is considered an employee of the corporation and his/her compensation (including salary and benefits) is treated the same as for any other employee of the corporation. All normal employee benefits are available to the owner/employee.

Salary for the stockholder/employee must be considered reasonable (neither too high nor too low) as loosely defined by the federal tax regulations. Discussion of "reasonableness" is beyond the scope of this book, and you should talk to your accountant about this issue.

Health insurance paid for a stockholder who has more than 2% ownership is recorded as health insurance expense in the business' books as for any other employee, but there are complicated tax reporting issues for this benefit. Payroll tax consequences for this benefit should be discussed with your accountant and, if applicable, your outside payroll service.

Additionally, the corporation's tax return preparer needs to know the amounts of health insurance paid for each applicable stockholder so that the appropriate tax reporting can be transferred to Form 1120S and to each stockholder's Schedule K-1.

WARNING: The IRS takes a dim view of active stockholder/employees taking no payroll while receiving other benefits from the business.

An S Corporation can also pay directors' fees to owners actively serving on its Board of Directors in compensation for their oversight of the business. These payments are usually tied to attendance at Board meetings. They are paid like subcontractor fees (for which Form 1099 is issued) and are recorded as a charge to the Directors Fee Expense account. This fee is tax deductible by the corporation. Directors' fees for an S Corporation are recorded the same as for a C Corporation, as discussed earlier in the section on C Corporations.

Draws From S Corporations

Distributions taken from the business by its stockholders are treated as draws (like partners in a partnership), using the postings shown in Table 7-16.

Account	Debit	Credit
3501 –Draw Stockholder A	500.00	
3502 –Draw Stockholder B	300.00	
3503 –Draw Stockholder C	200.00	
1000 – Bank Account		1000.00

Table 7-16: Track stockholder draws in individual equity accounts for each stockholder.

The equity of an S Corporation is required to be allocated among its stockholders and needs to remain in proportion to the percentage of stock each stockholder owns. Annually, the operating income and expenses are allocated to the stockholders according to their percentage of stock ownership. This action increases and decreases their individual equity balances.

Equity is also reduced by each stockholder's distributions. Any items of draw that are not in proportion to stock ownership need to be corrected within the next fiscal year by issuing catch up distributions to adjust the balances to their proper individual percentages according to stock ownership.

S Corporation Taxation

An S Corporation files its own corporate tax return (Form 1120S), which is similar to a partnership's tax return. The S Corporation provides each of its stockholders with a Schedule K-1 that includes each stockholder's share of net business income and several other classes of income, expenses, and credits that the stockholders report on their personal tax returns. When profit is taxed to the individual stockholder, but the total amount is not withdrawn, the undrawn amount is available for withdrawal at a later date with no income tax consequence.

Chapter 8

Inventory

An inventory item is a physical product you manufacture or purchase for the purpose of reselling to a customer. The main types of businesses that track inventory are manufacturers, wholesale distributors, and retailers. If you drop-ship to customers from a manufacturer or distributor, you don't track inventory because it's not your warehouse that's being tracked for inventory quantities and value.

Things you buy to sell to customers in the normal course of business with those customers usually aren't tracked as inventory. This means that if you're an electrician and you buy wire, outlets, and various electrical parts that you sell to your customers as part of a job, you usually don't have to track those parts as inventory. On the other hand, a contractor with ten trucks, each carrying $10,000 in supplies/parts, might have to report inventory. If you fit that definition (or the amount of stock you have on trucks and/or in a warehouse comes close to that definition), ask your accountant if the amount still in stock at the end of the year is significant enough to add inventory to your tax return.

Tracking Inventory Items

Every individual inventory item in your warehouse must be tracked carefully. That's the only way to make sure every customer gets exactly the inventory item ordered, and your supplier sends you exactly what you ordered. More important, it's the only way to make sure the financial data is accurate (the quantity and value of your inventory items).

NOTE: Many small businesses don't have real warehouses; instead inventory is stored in a garage, a shed, a back room, the basement, or some combination of those places. When I use the word "warehouse" I mean any location in which you store your inventory.

Naming Inventory Parts

Each inventory part you stock must have a unique code or name. Some businesses use "English" (such as Widget) and other businesses use numbers or a combination of letters or numbers (such as Wid97).

In addition to the code/name, create a description of the item. For many inventory items, it's helpful to create a description for sales and a separate description for purchases, because the descriptions are often different. Customer descriptions tend to be plain English (e.g. Widget), while the purchase description matches the text your supplier uses (e.g. Widget88897).

TIP: If you create a catalog or printed price list for your customers, make sure the content of that document uses the code/name you're using in your inventory tracking. That way, when customers want to place an order, you don't have to spend time translating the order into your official inventory tracking codes, and you can be sure the customer receives the item that's expected.

Tracking Inventory Locations

Sometimes, businesses with a great deal of inventory have to split the inventory into multiple locations. Some businesses use multiple locations to store specific inventory items in one place and other specific inventory items in another place. Other businesses (those with multiple locations) store a full set of inventory items in each place.

NOTE: Businesses with a single location often track the location of each inventory item by shelf number or bin number.

Tracking location makes it easier to find inventory when you're filling an order, as well as making it easier to count your inventory accurately.

Some accounting software provides location tracking. Unfortunately, neither QuickBooks nor Peachtree accounting (two popular programs for small businesses) can track multiple locations. You'll either have to purchase an add-on or keep location information outside of your accounting software.

However, if you have only one location for inventory and you want to be able to track the shelf/bin number for each item, both of those programs provide a feature called "Custom Fields" and you can create a custom field to track that information.

Tracking Important Inventory Data

Depending on the type of inventory items you sell, there may be other important data you need to track for each item:

- Lot Numbers
- Serial Numbers

- Manufacturer's Part Number
- Default Vendor

All high-end (expensive) accounting software programs manage serial numbers. However, of the two popular programs for small businesses (Peachtree and QuickBooks), only Peachtree manages serial numbers.

Inventory Accounting Tasks

The way you track financial data for buying and selling inventory items differs greatly from the way you track other purchases and sales.

When you purchase office supplies, you write a check and post the check to an expense named Office Supplies. Your Profit & Loss statement includes that expense, which reduces your taxable income. The same is true of rent, payroll, advertising, utilities, and most of your other purchases/expenses.

Inventory doesn't work the same way. Here are the guidelines for understanding accounting for inventory:

- Purchasing inventory (including inventory parts for manufacturing) is not an expense.

- Inventory is an asset.

- The value of your inventory asset is based on its cost, not its retail value.

- When an inventory product is sold, the expense (the cost of the inventory item) is posted and the value of the inventory asset is decreased by the same amount.

Creating Accounts for Inventory Accounting

In order to perform accounting tasks for inventory, you need several posting accounts devoted to inventory transactions:

- Inventory Asset, an asset of the type Current Asset.

- Cost of Goods Sold (COGS), an expense account (a specific type of expense account; it appears before "regular" expenses in the Profit & Loss statement).

- Inventory Adjustments, which can either be an expense account or a COGS account (ask your accountant which type of account to use).

In the following sections I'll explain when and how each of these accounts is involved in inventory transactions. Walking through the steps often makes it easier to understand the rather complicated accounting rules for inventory.

Purchasing Inventory

When you buy inventory to resell, or to create a manufactured product, the check you write is posted to the inventory asset, as seen in Table 8-1.

Account	Debit	Credit
1500 – Inventory Asset	5024.00	
1000 – Bank Account		5024.00

Table 8-1: Purchasing inventory isn't an expense; instead, you're buying an asset.

The amount you enter is the total amount of the vendor's bill. This includes inbound shipping, sales tax, handling charges, and any other charges included in the bill. Do not separate the actual product cost from the other costs; post the total cost to the inventory asset account. The cost of your inventory includes everything you're charged to receive the inventory items.

NOTE: If you have a sales tax license be sure your suppliers have a copy of it so you aren't charged sales tax for any items you purchase for resale.

If you enter a vendor bill for later payment instead of writing a check, the posting is slightly different. As you can see in Table 8-2, the inventory asset is still increased (a debit), but the credit side is applied to Accounts Payable.

Account	Debit	Credit
1500 – Inventory Asset	5024.00	
2100 – Accounts Payable		5024.00

Table 8-2: If you enter the vendor's bill instead of writing a direct check, the amount is posted to A/P.

When you pay the bill, A/P is reduced (debited) and your bank account is reduced (credited) by the amount of the payment.

Tracking the Quantity and Value of Inventory Items

In addition to buying inventory and posting it to the inventory asset account, you must track the quantity and cost of your purchase.

If you use accounting software, this is automatic; the data is part of the purchase and sales transactions. If you aren't using accounting software you must maintain the quantity and cost manually (such as in Excel).

Enter the total quantity purchased and the total cost. Then divide the total cost by the quantity to get the cost of each individual item. For example, if you purchased 30 widgets for a total cost of $5024.00 (including all shipping, tax, handling charges, etc. from the vendor), the cost of each widget is $167.47.

It doesn't matter if the vendor's catalog says that each widget is $158.00. You determine the cost based on the vendor's charge to you (which may include sales tax, shipping, and other costs). When you divide the total charge by the quantity received, you know it cost you $167.47 to bring in this item and that is your cost of the item. The cost per item is posted to COGS when you sell the item (covered in the section "Selling Inventory", later in this chapter).

Using Purchase Orders

You can use a purchase order (PO) to order inventory items from your suppliers; in fact, many vendors require a PO When you receive the bill, the PO number is on the bill.

A PO has no effect on your financial records. No amounts are posted to any account. Purchase orders are merely documents; they exist only to help you track what you've ordered so you can match your order against the items you receive, and so you can tell whether more stock is due to arrive when the quantity of an item is low. You create the financial transaction when the vendor's bill arrives.

If you use accounting software, POs are a built-in feature. When the inventory arrives, you can open the PO and create a vendor invoice automatically. If only some of your order arrives, the items still waiting remain on the PO where they are marked as "still open". When the rest of the order arrives, you finish receiving against the PO. If the missing items aren't going to be shipped to you, you can close the PO and the outstanding quantity disappears.

In a manual system, you can use a pre-printed form or a Microsoft Word document to create a PO. Each PO must have a unique number. Track the PO number and its details in Excel as seen in Figure 8-1.

	Date	Vendor	Item	Qty	Cost Per	PO Total	QtyRecd	Total Amt Due	Closed?
15	02/05/10	DVS	Widget	20	155.20	3,104.00	20	3,142.20	Y
16	02/18/10	RRD	Thingy	10	185.00	1,850.00	10	1,871.65	Y
17	03/21/10	DVS	Gadget	5	206.00	1,030.00	5	1,060.33	Y
18	04/16/10	DVS	Widget	25	155.20	3,880.00	15	2,378.12	N
19	06/10/10	LMN	DooDad	60	11.00	660.00	60	681.95	Y
20	06/28/10	RRD	Thingy	8	185.00	1,480.00	8	1,491.90	Y

Figure 8-1: Track PO details to make sure you know what items are due to arrive and which have arrived.

Selling Inventory

An inventory item becomes an expense instead of an asset when you sell it. The expense is posted to an account named Cost of Goods Sold. (The name of that expense account is a reminder that you can't expense the cost of purchasing the inventory item until you sell it – the account isn't named Cost of Goods **Purchased**, it's Cost of Goods **Sold**.)

When you sell a customer an inventory item, you take the item out of inventory (reducing the value of your inventory asset account) and post the cost of the item to COGS (increasing your expenses). In addition, you post the income.

The total of the sale is not affected by the postings to the inventory asset and COGS accounts; these accounts wash (zero themselves out). What happens is that the value of the inventory you sold is moved from the asset to the expense.

Let's say you sell a customer two of those widgets that cost you $167.47 each. You've priced the widgets at $190.00 each. Table 8-3 displays the postings for a simple cash sale of those widgets.

Account	Debit	Credit
4000 – Product Sales		380.00
1500 – Inventory Asset		334.94
4900 – Cost of Goods Sold	334.94	
1000 – Bank Account	380.00	

Table 8-3: Posting journal for a simple cash sale of inventory items.

The sale of inventory items can be more complex than this simple cash sale. You might create an invoice instead of receiving cash, you might charge the customer for shipping, and the items and shipping might be taxable. Table 8-4 shows the posting journal for a more complex sale; notice that the Inventory Asset and COGS postings are the same as for the simple cash sale and don't affect the amount due from the customer.

Account	Debit	Credit
4000 – Product Sales		380.00
2200 – Sales Tax Payable		31.20
4090 – Shipping Income		10.00
1500 – Inventory Asset		334.94
4900 – Cost of Goods Sold	334.94	
1100 – Accounts Receivable	421.20	

Table 8-4: Posting journal for an invoiced sale of inventory items.

Valuation Methods for Inventory

There are several methods available for calculating the value of each inventory item. The common methods are:

- Average Cost
- FIFO (First In, First Out)
- LIFO (Last In, First Out)
- Specific Identification

Most accounting software that supports inventory is able to calculate inventory values for every method. Of the two accounting programs popular with small businesses (QuickBooks and Peachtree), only Peachtree offers all of these methods. QuickBooks only supports average cost.

WARNING: Talk to your accountant before selecting a valuation method. The method you choose is global; it's part of the setup and configuration of your accounting software as well as your tax returns. You can't choose one method for some inventory items and a different method for other inventory items.

The first time you buy any inventory item, it's easy to determine the cost: Divide the total cost by the total quantity to get the cost per item. In the widget purchase discussed in the previous section, it was easy to calculate the cost of each widget at $167.47: the vendor's charge for 30 widgets was $5024.00 (including all shipping, tax, handling charges, etc.).

After you sell 25 of the 30 widgets, you order 30 more. But the cost has changed and now the vendor's charge for 30 widgets is $5563.00. You have 35 widgets in stock; what's the cost per widget? Suppose the price changes quite a bit every time you purchase the item; sometimes it's lower than the last time and sometimes it's higher than the last time?

What amount do you post to COGS if you sell a single widget? What amount do you post to COGS if you sell 30 widgets?

The answer is, "It depends on the method you're using for determining the value of inventory items". In the following section I'll give an overview of each of the four valuation methods I listed at the beginning of this section.

Average Cost

The traditional average cost method takes the total amount spent on the inventory item and divides it by the total number of units purchased. If you're using accounting software, the calculations that track average cost are automatic.

If you track inventory manually, a simple Excel spreadsheet can track the average cost of each inventory item, as seen in Figure 8-2.

	A	B	C	D
	InventoryCosts.xls			
1	Date	Qty	Amount Spent	Avg Cost This Purchase
2	01/15/10	30	$5,024.00	$167.47
3	02/10/10	30	$5,563.00	$185.43
4	03/30/10	20	$3,524.40	$176.22
5	05/20/10	25	$4,186.75	$167.47
6				
7	Current Avg Cost	105	$18,298.15	$174.27
8	Gadget / Thingys \ Widget /			

Figure 8-2: Track the average cost by entering the details of each purchase.

The formulas in the spreadsheet are quite simple (in fact, most accounting software programs use these formulas to calculate the current average cost automatically):

- Column D is Column C divided by Column B (e.g. =C2/B2).

- The last row (the running calculation for the current average cost) SUMs Column B and Column C. The formula for Column D remains the same as the other rows (C/B).

If you use QuickBooks, the formula for calculating average cost is not the same as the formula I just described. Instead of tracking purchases and quantity purchased, QuickBooks uses the following formula: **Total current asset value of the item divided by the current quantity on hand**.

The QuickBooks formula isn't wrong; that is, it isn't against the rules of Generally Accepted Accounting Procedures. However, it isn't as desirable as the common formula. (The seriousness of the problem with the QuickBooks formula increases if the item is expensive and the price changes frequently. The effect on your Balance Sheet and your Profit & Loss Statement could be significant.)

An inexpensive add-on for QuickBooks that improves average costing is available from **www.beyondtheledgers.com**. On the Products page, look for Inventory Cost Adjuster. This program calculates the average cost of inventory items using the common average costing method and integrates the results into your QuickBooks company file.

FIFO (First In, First Out)

FIFO tracks the quantity and amount of each purchase in chronological order. As you sell inventory, the cost of that inventory is posted against those "purchase lots". FIFO sells off inventory sequentially, starting with inventory from the oldest purchase, and moving through the next purchase, the purchase after that, and so on. The cost of the item is taken from each set of purchases.

For example, let's say you purchased 30 widgets at a cost of $167.47/widget in January. As you sell the widgets (at a price of $190.00 per widget), the COGS account is increased and the inventory asset account is decreased by the amount of the purchase cost. The income account is increased for the sales price for the widgets. The bank account or A/R (depending on whether it's a cash sale or an invoiced sale) is increased by the sales price for the widgets.

If you sell exactly 30 widgets before you purchase the next set of widgets at a cost of $150.20 per widget, the next widget sale uses the new cost to post amounts to COGS and the inventory asset accounts.

Of course, it rarely works that neatly. The odds are that you'll have at least several of the January widgets left when you purchase more in February. Let's say you have 4 widgets from the January purchase in stock, and 30 widgets from the February purchase in stock. Now a customer buys 6 widgets. When you create the sales transaction (charging the customer $190.00 per widget), the posting journal resembles Table 8-5.

Account	Debit	Credit
4000 – Product Sales		1140.00
1500 – Inventory Asset		970.28
4900 – Cost of Goods Sold	970.28	
1000 – Bank Account	1140.00	

Table 8-5: FIFO separates the cost per purchase to post amounts to the COGS and inventory asset accounts.

The amount of $970.28 that is posted to the COGS and inventory asset accounts is a result of the following calculation:

- 4 widgets @ 167.47 = 669.88
- 2 widgets @ 150.20 = 300.40

As you continue to buy and sell widgets, the postings to the COGS and inventory asset accounts are calculated on a First In, First Out cost basis. This is a complicated procedure, difficult to do manually. Good software is the answer to maintaining FIFO.

You can change the price of the item (usually you raise the price because your costs increased) without affect the postings to the COGS and inventory asset accounts. If you raise the price before you sell off the oldest purchase lot, that just increases your profit for that lot.

You don't have to store the items by FIFO; it doesn't matter unless you're selling food or other date-sensitive products (in which case you're also tracking lot numbers and dates). Store the items from all your purchases together and just pull the quantity needed for each sale from the group.

If you're using QuickBooks and your accountant feels that FIFO is better suited for your business, you can buy an inexpensive QuickBooks add-on named FIFO Calculator from *www.beyondtheledgers.com*. This add-on reads your transactions for inventory items and calculates inventory valuation as FIFO instead of average cost. The results are reported in Microsoft Excel. The program produces detailed reports for all inventory items, showing FIFO value calculation for each inventory transaction that affects valuation. Your accountant can use this data to adjust your general ledger and prepare your tax returns.

LIFO (Last In, First Out)

LIFO is appropriate if you sell the most recently purchased products first. The cost of the item is calculated in the opposite direction from FIFO. LIFO posts costs in reverse order of your purchase history because each sale is matched against the latest product purchase. Over time, if you haven't been purchasing new items regularly, COGS and the inventory asset postings could be calculated using the first purchase of the item (perhaps a long long time ago).

The processes involved in calculating costs with LIFO are the same as those described in the previous section on FIFO, but in reverse chronological order. Like FIFO, this is a complicated mathematical process and works best with good software. FIFO is less common than LIFO, especially in small businesses.

Specific Identification

Specific identification is a valuation method in which each physical inventory item has its own inventory name/code and has its own cost. When you sell the item, that cost is posted to the COGS and inventory asset accounts. (This means you have a profit/loss report for each individual sale.)

The specific identification valuation method is used for "made to order" products, such as expensive hand-made jewelry, or other unique products. Your inventory list contains every product, and each individual product has a quantity of 1 as well as a unique item name/code.

Each individual product is received into inventory with its specific cost, and when the product is sold the quantity goes to zero and it cannot be sold again (if another customer wants an identical product you have to receive that new product into inventory with a different name/code).

Most accounting software programs that support average cost, FIFO, and LIFO also support specific identification. Peachtree, a popular program for small businesses, supports specific identification but insists on a serial number for each product (there's a serial number field in the inventory record). If you don't put serial numbers on your products, you can invent a number; a common workaround is the date the product was put into inventory such as 20100515 for Year 2010 Month 05 Day 15 (May 15, 2010).

Manufacturing Assembled Products

Manufacturing businesses buy parts and then use those parts to create a new product; it's the new product that they sell to customers. When you buy parts to create a new product, the common term for the end product is *an assembly* or *a build*. (I tend to favor the term assembly and that's the term I use in this discussion.)

The business process for manufacturers differs from wholesale and retail businesses that buy inventory items and resell them to customers. The process for manufacturers is "buy the parts, build the product". The process for wholesale and retail businesses is "buy it, mark it up, sell it".

When you manufacture an assembly from parts, both the parts and the finished product are tracked as inventory. In essence, you move all the items required for the product out of inventory when you build the assembly, and then bring the finished product into inventory. Usually, the value of your inventory asset doesn't change because you've merely "swapped" the cost of the items from "individual inventory items" to "parts of an assembly inventory item". However, the quantities of the items change because the quantity on hand of the individual items is reduced and the quantity on hand of the assembly is increased.

Creating a Bill of Materials

A bill of materials (commonly abbreviated *BOM*) is a list of the components needed to build an assembly. The BOM also tracks the cost of the components, creating a total cost for the assembled product.

The BOM always contains the individual inventory items that are needed, along with the quantity of each item. In addition, a BOM can contain the following types of components:

- Items used for the purpose of completing the process of building the assembly, such as nails, screws, rivets, staples, etc. These items are usually not tracked as inventory because they're bought in bulk (making it onerous to count them) and are used only for the purpose of physically creating the assembly.

- Items used for the purpose of packing the assembly, such as boxes, padding, tape, labels, etc. These items are also not tracked as inventory.

- Labor (time) used for the process of building the assembly.

You need to track the non-inventory costs so you know what it costs to build the product. Then you can set the price for the product. Table 8-6 is a representation of a BOM that has inventory parts as well as other types of components.

Item	Description	Type	Qty	Cost	Tot Cost
89998	Motor	Inventory	1	86.20	86.20
77764	Cabinet	Inventory	1	35.21	35.21
55590	Bezel	Inventory	4	10.00	40.00
	Screws	Misc	10	.20	2.00
	Washers	Misc	10	.10	1.00
	Labor	Time	1	14.00	14.00
	Box	Misc	1	2.10	2.10
TOTAL					180.51

Table 8-6: Common format of a Bill of Materials

Adjusting Inventory for Assemblies

When you build an assembly, the inventory items in the BOM are removed from inventory. This reduces the quantity on hand and also reduces the amount of the inventory asset by the cost of the inventory items in the assembled product.

Simultaneously, the process of building the assembly increases the quantity on hand of the assembled product and increases the balance of the inventory asset using the cost of the assembly (which includes the cost of the inventory items in the BOM). If the BOM includes only the inventory items, it's a straight swap; the amounts wash each other out. If the BOM has additional components, the inventory asset account is increased by the amount of the inventory items used plus the other costs.

If you refer back to the BOM that appears in the previous section, you can see that the cost of the assembly is $180.51. The cost of the inventory components totals $161.41. When you build this product the inventory asset account has the following postings:

- The account is reduced (credited) in the amount of $161.41 to post the removal of inventory items from stock.

- The account is increased (debited) in the amount of $180.51 to post the receipt of the assembly into inventory. That amount includes the inventory items as well as the supplies and labor used to make the assembled item.

If you're not using software that manages assemblies, you must perform these adjustments differently:

- You adjust the inventory items manually (which does not change the balance of the inventory asset account).

- You adjust the original expense account to which you posted the non-inventory components to move that cost into inventory (credit the expense and debit the inventory asset account).

Accounting software that supports building assemblies and BOM functions does all of this automatically. Tracking this manually is difficult and I wouldn't advise a manufacturing business to try to manage this process without software.

Selling an Assembled Product

When you sell an assembled inventory product the postings are the same as they would be if you were selling an individual inventory item (using the current cost of the assembled product). For the same assembled product I discussed in the previous sections, Table 8-7 displays the posting journal for a sale of the assembled product at a price of $250.00.

Account	Debit	Credit
4000 – Product Sales		250.00
1500 – Inventory Asset		180.51
4900 – Cost of Goods Sold	180.51	
1000 – Bank Account	250.00	

Table 8-7: Postings for sales of assembled products are the same as postings for individual inventory items.

Adjusting Inventory

There are a variety of scenarios that require an adjustment to your inventory numbers. The most common is that the result of counting the inventory doesn't match the quantity on hand in your inventory records. All accounting software that supports inventory has a built-in feature for adjusting the quantity and value of each inventory item.

Counting Inventory

Counting inventory can be a complicated, time-consuming, boring process. However, it's imperative that you periodically perform a physical count of all your inventory items. At minimum you must count inventory yearly, but many accountants suggest more frequent counts. (If you have a great many inventory items, periodically count groups of items if counting all of your inventory at a single time is too time consuming).

Your inventory count and the quantity on hand reported by your accounting data must match. Following are some guidelines to follow that could make this process easier and more efficient.

Create an Inventory Count Worksheet

Print a worksheet that lists every inventory item and has a space for entering the count. Most accounting software has a worksheet available for this purpose, but you can create your own worksheet in Excel. Figure 8-3 displays the minimum information contained in most inventory count worksheets.

Inventory Count Worksheet

		Item Code	On Hand	Physical Count
	Inventory			
		Axles	5	
		CableSet	2	
		Casings	6	
		Cogs	8	
		Doohickeys	6	
		Dowels	9	
		Gadget01	6	
		Gadget02	8	
		Ratchets	6	
		Sound Card	6	
		Thingys	5	
		Wheels	0	
		Widgets	84	
	Assembly			
		Kit-01	3	
		Kit-02	2	
		Kit-03	1	
		Kit-05	0	

Figure 8-3: Use a worksheet to enter the quantity you find on the shelves.

If you track bins, shelf numbers, or other location data, display that information on the worksheet. In fact, it's best to sort by location to make it easier for the people doing the counting to find the items.

If you have a lot of inventory and multiple counters, print a master sheet as a reference and then print the appropriate section for each counter. If your worksheet doesn't separate pages easily (some software worksheets don't allow page breaks), print a second copy of the worksheet and cut it so there's a section for each counter. As each person finishes counting and hands in the worksheet, copy those numbers to the master sheet so all the numbers are in one place.

TIP: If you use software that lets you make inventory items inactive, and doesn't print inactive items on the worksheet (e.g. QuickBooks), make all your items active before printing the worksheet. Items are often inactive because they're seasonal, or because you've temporarily stopped selling them for some other reason, but inactive items may have quantities in stock and they must be counted.

Freeze Inventory Activity During the Count

While you're counting inventory, you can't remove items and you can't bring in items. That's true for your accounting records and it's also true for your physical activities regarding inventory items. You have to freeze all sales and receipt of inventory transactions.

Most accounting software that supports inventory has a "freeze" feature built in. You can create invoices and cash sales, you can receive against purchase orders, and you can record the vendor's bill. All of those transactions are kept in a "holding file" until you tell the software the physical count is completed. At that point, those transactions enter the software and the software prints an "adjusting report" so you can use those transactions as you make your inventory adjustments after the physical count.

QuickBooks and Peachtree, the two most popular programs for small businesses, lack a "freeze" function, so you have to create a workaround. Create sales and inventory receipt transactions on paper, using a word processor. Print each transaction. Don't unpack and shelve any inventory that's delivered during the count. When the count is finished and the inventory adjustment is entered, then enter the transactions in your software and stock your shelves.

Adjust Inventory Quantities After the Count

When the count is finished, use the numbers in the physical count column of the worksheet to create an inventory adjustment. If you use software, there's a transaction window to do this. Go through each inventory item in the window and enter the "new" quantity. The software automatically adjusts the quantity and attendant asset value of each item (using the current cost of the item).

- Software inventory adjustment functions automatically replace the total value of your inventory in the inventory asset account with the new total.

- If you track inventory in Excel and you replace the existing quantity with the new quantity, be sure there's a column on each item's row that contains the current cost for each item. Create a formula (quantity x cost) on each row to calculate the new value of each inventory item. Then calculate the total of that column to get the new asset value for your inventory.

For either scenario, you need to post the new total inventory value into your inventory asset account. This is essentially a journal entry (even if your software has an adjustment transaction window) involving two accounts:

- The inventory asset account.

- The inventory adjustment account.

NOTE: The inventory adjustment account may be an Expense or a Cost of Goods Sold account, depending on your accountant's advice.

If the physical count resulted in more inventory than the records in your books, the inventory adjustment increases (debits) the inventory asset account and decreases (credits) the inventory adjustment account.

If the physical count resulted in fewer inventories than the records in your books, the inventory adjustment decreases (credits) the inventory asset account and increases (debits) the inventory adjustment account.

If the physical count matched the records in your books, you don't have to do anything (but that almost never happens).

Adjusting Inventory for Damaged Goods

Sometimes inventory items are damaged, and can't be sold. That makes them worthless, so you can't count them as an asset (as part of the inventory asset account). Additionally, you've lost the chance to sell the item so you want to turn the cost of the item into an expense.

Essentially, inventory adjustments for damaged goods are journal entries, exactly like the journal entry that takes place when you adjust inventory after a physical count. The two accounts used in the journal entry are the inventory asset account and the inventory adjustment account.

Because you're adjusting for damaged goods, you are reducing the amount of the inventory asset and increasing the inventory adjustment account, as seen in Table 8-8. The amount of the adjustment is the current cost of the item.

Account	Debit	Credit
1500 – Inventory Asset		95.00
5010 - Inventory Adjustment	95.00	

Table 8-8: Damaged goods reduce the value of your inventory asset.

If you're keep inventory records manually, don't forget to reduce the quantity on hand; accounting software does this automatically in the inventory adjustment transaction window.

Crediting Customers for Damaged Goods

If a customer discovered the damage, you owe the customer a credit (or a refund) for the price of the damaged goods. A credit is the opposite of a sale, of course, so it reduces income and reduces A/R. In addition, sales tax the customer paid is credited and removed from the sales tax liability account. (Chapter 3 explains and illustrates the postings for customer credits.)

If you can return the item to the manufacturer, have the customer return the inventory to you so you can return it for a credit or refund. (You'll have to add the money the customer spends for shipping to the credit memo).

If the manufacturer won't take the item back, or if you're the manufacturer, it saves you the cost of shipping if you tell the customer you'll issue the credit memo without the need to return the item.

NOTE: You create the customer credit in addition to removing the item with the inventory adjustment explained in the previous section.

QuickBooks and Peachtree use items in all customer transactions, including customer credit transactions. Because the credit is for an inventory item, the software brings the item back into inventory. After you issue the credit, do an inventory adjustment as described in the previous section to remove the item from inventory.

Creating a Vendor Credit for Damaged Goods

When you return damaged goods to the vendor, the transaction reduces your A/P liability and reduces the value of your inventory asset, as seen in Table 8-9.

Account	Debit	Credit
1500 – Inventory Asset		95.00
2100 – Accounts Payable	95.00	

Table 8-9: Take the damaged part out of inventory and reduce your A/P liability.

Adjusting Inventory for "Freebies"

You must also adjust inventory when you remove inventory without selling it. Use the same inventory adjustment process described earlier for adjusting quantity after a physical count, but change the adjustment account as follows:

- If you send free products (samples) to customers, use your Advertising or Marketing expense account.

- If you provide an inventory product to a nonprofit organization, use your Charitable Contributions expense account.

- If you take inventory off the shelf in order to use it in your business, use your Office Expenses expense account.

Some or all of these "freebies" may require the payment of use tax, depending on your state's tax law. See Chapter 6 to learn about tracking use tax liability.

Work In Process

Work in Process (commonly referred to as *WIP*) is an accounting concept that tracks resources that have been allocated to the process of building assembled products. The WIP account is a Current Asset account.

The Theory of Work In Process

The theory behind WIP is that when you know you're about to build new products you should reserve the components needed in your WIP account. This means that inventory items are transferred from inventory to WIP. Sometimes other components such as labor, non-inventory materials, and anything else that will be used to produce the finished product are posted to the WIP account.

WIP is used in large manufacturing companies, and usually the WIP account represents components that are waiting for everything to arrive in order to begin building the assembled products. Inherent in most WIP tracking is "delay"; one or more components are missing.

Frequently the missing components are "pre-builds" – assembled products that aren't sold to customers; instead they are used in the finished assembled product. In order to build the finished product you have to build the pre-builds. In addition, some components may not be on hand; either they're en route or they haven't yet been ordered. WIP account balances are usually quite large because companies that use this account invest large amounts of money in components, and manufacture large quantities of assembled products from these components.

WIP Redefined for Small Businesses

For small businesses, a WIP account is useful for tracking the costs of an inventory product that is created instead of purchased. The individual parts and services that are needed to create the product are purchased specifically to create the product. You don't need to track those parts as inventory because they're never going to be offered for sale; they exist only to produce another product.

For example, some businesses purchase individual items and improve or repair those items before offering them for sale. Antique dealers, furniture restorers, antique car dealers, and other similar businesses are a few examples.

Other businesses create an item by purchasing specialized services along with some parts. The services are specific to the creation of the inventory item, and the parts are never sold; they exist only to produce the finished product. For example, anyone who produces media such as books, CDs, videos, etc. purchases services and items over a period of time before merging everything into the finished product.

Tracking Production Costs in WIP

When you have components that are never sold to customers because they exist only to create a product, instead of creating an assembled product you can post the costs to a WIP account. When the product is ready to sell, receive the product into inventory using the total expenses as the cost of the inventory item. For example, Table 8-10 represents posting journals for a series of payments for the purchase of services and items needed to create a product (in this case a restored car).

Date	Account	Debit	Credit	Memo
4/15/10	1000 – Bank Account		3000.00	Old Junker
4/15/10	1550 – WIP	3000.00		Old Junker
5/22/10	1000 – Bank Account		150.00	Body Filler
5/22/10	1550 – WIP	150.00		Body Filler
6/15/10	1000 – Bank Account		400.00	Fenders-lights
6/15/10	1550 – WIP	400.00		Fenders-lights
6/28/10	1000 – Bank Account		1000.00	Painting Service
6/28/10	1550 – WIP	1000.00		Painting Service
7/14/10	1000 – Bank Account		820.00	Upholstery Service
7/14/10	1550 – WIP	820.00		Upholstery Service
7/21/10	1000 – Bank Account		180.00	Tune-up
7/21/10	1550 – WIP	180.00		Tune-up

Table 8-10: Track the costs of creating a product in a WIP account.

You can use WIP for the same purpose even if you're not creating a single unique item. This works just as well for producing large quantities of an inventory item. As an example, Table 8-11 shows the postings for goods and services purchased to create thousands of copies of a book.

Date	Account	Debit	Credit	Memo
2/14/10	1550 - WIP	1200.00		Editor
2/14/10	1000 – Bank Account		1200.00	Editor
3/29/10	1550 – WIP	1100.00		Artist – cover
3/29/10	1000 – Bank Account		1100.00	Artist – cover
4/10/10	1550 – WIP	1600.00		Printer file production
4/10/10	1000 – Bank Account		1600.00	Printer file production
4/22/10	1550 – WIP	1000.00		Color separations
4/22/10	1000 – Bank Account		1000.00	Color separations
4/29/10	1550 – WIP	6000.00		Paper
4/29/10	1000 – Bank Account		6000.00	Paper
5/10/10	1550 – WIP	2100.00		Plate & presswork
5/10/10	1000 – Bank Account		2100.00	Plate & presswork
5/15/10	1550 – WIP	8000.00		Printing & binding
5/15/10	1000 – Bank Account		8000.00	Printing & binding
5/20/10	1550 – WIP	700.00		Shipping to warehouse
5/20/10	1000 – Bank Account		700.00	Shipping to warehouse

Table 8-11: You can track outsourced work and supplies in WIP when you're creating inventory items.

Moving WIP into Inventory

When the product is ready to sell, you receive it into inventory using the total posted to WIP as the cost of the inventory. You also increase the quantity of the inventory item by the appropriate number.

This is really an inventory adjustment, similar to the inventory adjustments discussed earlier in this chapter. However, in this case the offsetting account for the inventory asset is the WIP account instead of the inventory adjustment account. Table 8-12 represents the posting journal for bringing 4,000 books into inventory by moving the WIP cost total into the inventory asset account.

Account	Debit	Credit
1500 – Inventory Asset	21700.00	
1550 – WIP		21700.00

Table 8-12: The funds expended for WIP have become the cost of the inventory being received.

You also must track the quantity received of the new inventory item, using the total cost divided by the quantity of items to determine the cost of each item. Accounting software does this automatically in a single inventory adjustment transaction.

Chapter 9

Payroll & Independent Contractors

Some businesses with employees do the payroll themselves (called *in-house* payroll processing), while other businesses hire a payroll service company to take care of payroll (called *outsourced* payroll processing). Every employee receives a W-2 at the end of the year.

When business owners view the financial reports for payroll postings, or view the government reports they have to sign, they frequently don't understand what they're looking at. Accountants receive a great many questions from business owners regarding the financial information for payroll, and in this chapter I'll explain the effects of payroll on your books.

Some businesses hire independent contractors instead of, or in addition to, employees. Independent contractors are paid an amount agreed upon in advance (and often there's a formal written agreement or contract). The independent contractor receives Form 1099 at the end of the year. In this chapter I also discuss the accounting tasks involved in tracking independent contractors.

Employee Vs. Independent Contractor

Most accountants will tell you that at some point they've had a conversation with clients who want to hire independent contractors instead of employees. The clients point out that hiring workers as independent contractors is less expensive and less complicated than hiring employees. That's true.

Accountants have to explain that the description of an independent contractor is defined by the IRS, not by the employer. The definition is rather rigid (and almost impossible to get around). If the IRS determines that the workers you've paid for years as independent contractors were really employees, the cost of catching up with unpaid liabilities and the attendant interest and penalties could be large enough to destroy your business.

I'm not going to go over all the rules and the entire fine points that the IRS uses in making a determination about a worker's status; instead I'll give you a brief overview. More information is available on the IRS website (http://www.irs. gov/). Following are some important questions to ask you.

Do you have the right to control what the worker does and how the worker does it?

Notice that I said "the right to control", which is not the same as asking, "do you control?" or "do you sometimes take the time to control?" Whether you exercise that right isn't the question; it's whether you and the worker both know that you have the right to control the work environment.

If you have the right to control what the worker does and direct how the worker does it, the worker is an employee.

If the worker is an independent contractor, the business has the right to control or direct only the **result** of the work and has no right to control the way the worker accomplishes the result. You don't set hours, you don't tell the worker where to work, and you don't have any control over the methods used by the worker.

Do you control the business and financial aspects of the worker's job?

The business and financial aspects of a worker's job include payment, providing tools and equipment, and other details (such as reimbursement of expenses).

If you decide the frequency of payment (e.g. you tell the worker, "We issue your check every Friday"), the IRS will probably determine that the worker is an employee. Most independent contractors present a payment schedule for the work they perform. Even if no formal payment schedule is presented, the frequency of payment for an independent contractor is determined by the agreement between you and the independent contractor (and if the payment schedule happens to be the same as your payroll schedule, that's a coincidence).

If you purchase and maintain the tools and equipment used by the worker, the IRS will almost certainly determine that the worker is an employee. Independent contractors usually have their own tools and equipment.

NOTE: A common "test" includes whether the worker can be doing similar work for others while doing work for you – having multiple customers for the same work is the mark of a true independent contractor.

If you always reimburse the worker for money expended on behalf of the business, the IRS will probably determine the worker is an employee. Usually, independent contractors consider out-of-pocket expenses when they present their rate; they deduct the expenses on their own tax returns. If an independent contractor prefers to be reimbursed by the business, that fact is included in the agreement and the independent contractor usually submits an invoice for the out-of-pocket expenses.

Are your workers requesting independent contractor status?

It doesn't matter. The IRS doesn't care about personal preferences. Neither your workers nor you get to decide based on the perceived financial advantages. If workers want to be deemed independent contractors, they need to perform their work the way independent contractors do. Their need to supply their own tools and equipment, maintain those tools and pieces of equipment (and, for some jobs, clothing or uniforms) and a commitment to getting each job done within a time frame mandated by an agreement between you and them. No more nine-to-five days where the unfinished work can wait until tomorrow.

Many employees who make this request think they'll gain more net funds as independent contractors who operate as a business. They see their gross pay rate and think they'd get to bank and keep that amount. It doesn't work that way. In fact, they often end up with less money than the net pay they receive as employees.

- Federal taxes aren't withheld, but they have to be paid when the independent contractor files taxes (the 1099 you send tells the IRS the gross amount they received). In fact, after the first year they have to send quarterly deposits against the federal income tax they'll owe.

- Medicare and social security aren't withheld, but they have to pay it; in fact, they have to pay double the amount of medicare and social security they're paying as employees (the employer matching amount is borne by the independent contractor).

- State income tax is due in the same amount it would be due as an employee.

- Local income taxes may be higher than the amount withheld for an employee. Many local taxing authorities levy taxes on business that aren't levied on employees. Usually, local tax authorities that impose wage taxes on employees impose a higher rate on businesses.

IRS publications on employee vs. independent contractor

You can learn more about the differences between employees and independent contractors by reading IRS Publication 1779, Independent Contractor or Employee. To get this article, enter the following URL in the Address Bar of your browser: **http://www.irs.gov/pub/irs-pdf/p1779.pdf**

Both employers and workers can ask the IRS to determine whether a specific individual is an independent contractor or an employee by filing Form SS-8 – Determination of Worker Status for Purposes of Federal Employment Taxes and Income Tax Withholding.

You can download Form SS-8 from the IRS website and mail it after you fill it in, or you can fill in the form online. The IRS uses the information in the form to work with you to determine the worker's status. Talk to your accountant before using the form.

Payroll

If you have employees, you have to create paychecks, track the liabilities and employer expenses related to those paychecks, and remit those liabilities and employer expenses. A great many postings to your general ledger take place as you perform these tasks. Even if you don't do your own payroll, you have to track those postings in your books (using the reports from your outside payroll company).

In the following sections I go over the accounting details that most business owners question their accountants about when they see payroll reports, Profit & Loss reports, Balance Sheet reports, and tax returns.

Gross and Net Pay

Everyone knows the difference between gross pay and net pay: Gross pay is your pay rate and net pay is the amount of your paycheck after all the deductions.

But, what's the difference in terms of your accounting books? Even if you outsource your payroll you have to enter the financial data in your books. Where and how do all the amounts get recorded? What else gets recorded? What's deductible on your tax return?

Gross Pay

Gross pay is the total due to an employee based on his/her pay rate, before any deductions. Gross pay is the amount you post to the expense account for salaries and wages. It doesn't matter how much money the employee actually receives, the gross pay is the tax deductible expense, and is usually posted to an expense account named Salaries & Wages.

If your business is a corporation, you must separate the gross pay expense for corporate officers from the gross pay entry for all other employees. A corporation's chart of accounts needs two expense accounts to track gross pay:

- Salaries – Officers
- Salaries & Wages – Other

Net Pay

Net pay is the amount of the paycheck an employee receives and it's the gross pay less the deductions. The amount of money deducted from employees' paychecks might stay in your bank account (albeit not for long) but you can't spend it because it isn't your money. These are your *payroll liabilities* and you have to remit the money to other entities.

NOTE: Net pay isn't posted to any payroll expense account; instead, it's posted to the bank account you use for payroll (as a check or as a direct deposit).

In addition to the money withheld from employees' checks, there are other payments related to payroll you have to send to other entities (covered in the following sections of this chapter). These are your *payroll expenses*.

NOTE: The money you spend on an outside payroll company isn't a payroll expense, it's an operating expense.

When you post your payroll, net pay is posted to the bank account. It's a credit to the bank account because it reduces the bank account balance. Table 9-1 is a simplified (actually, over-simplified) view of the way net pay is posted; the deductions and their postings are discussed in the following sections of this chapter.

Account	Debit	Credit
Salaries & Wages	5000.00	
Deductions from paychecks		2100.00
Bank account		2900.00

Table 9-1: The net pay is a credit to the bank account.

Payroll Liabilities

Payroll liabilities are defined the same way all liabilities are defined: A liability is something you have in your possession that doesn't belong to you; you're holding it for someone else. In this case, we refer to these liabilities as *payroll liabilities*.

All employers incur payroll liabilities for government agencies. Some employers also incur payroll liabilities for non-government entities such as insurance companies. The non-government liabilities depend on the benefits you provide for employees.

Payroll Liabilities for Tax Withholding

Government liabilities are those liabilities that are remitted to government agencies. The remittance always includes a form, even if the payment is remitted online. Your government payroll liabilities include the money withheld from employee paychecks as well as money due from you as the employer. The employer portion is turned into an expense and is covered in the section "Payroll Expenses". The liabilities for withholdings (called *trust fund taxes*) include some or all of the following:

- Federal income tax withheld from paychecks.
- Social security withheld from paychecks.

- Medicare withheld from paychecks.

- State income tax withheld from paychecks (if applicable).

- State unemployment tax withheld from paychecks (if applicable)

- State disability tax withheld from paychecks (if applicable)

- Local income tax withheld from paychecks (if applicable).

Social security withholdings have a limit; once the employee reaches a maximum gross pay for the year, social security is no longer withheld. (The maximum gross pay amount changes yearly.)

Some state taxes for unemployment and disability have a yearly maximum gross pay limit, after which tax is no longer due. Sometimes the limit is only applied to the employee, while other states apply a limit only to the employer (a payroll expense).

Payroll Liabilities for Employee Benefits

In addition to government liabilities, the benefits you provide employees may involve deductions from their paychecks. The withheld funds are sent to the applicable vendor, usually an insurance company and pension plan provider. Following are some of the common withholdings for benefits that small businesses offer:

- Contribution to medical benefits withheld.

- Contribution to retirement plan withheld.

- Contribution to health/legal savings plan withheld.

The company may also contribute to these benefits, and those contributions are posted as expenses (covered later in this chapter).

Other Withholding Liabilities

In addition to withholdings for taxes and benefits, your employees may have money withheld for other reasons. The two common withholding categories that are neither taxes nor benefits are:

- Contributions to charitable organizations.
- Garnishments.

Withholding for Charitable Contributions

If your employees have contributions withheld for a charitable organization, you remit the donation periodically. Many businesses offer a matching amount to these withheld funds (or a partial match), and those matching funds are an expense (posted to Charitable Contributions).

Withholding for Garnishments

A garnishment is a legal obligation owed by an employee that puts you in the middle of the employee's personal affairs. Garnishments are complicated and time consuming to administer, but they can't be avoided. If a garnishment order is delivered (paperwork is received from a federal, state, or local agency), employers are required to collect the garnished amount and remit it to the appropriate agency on behalf of the employee.

If you have a garnishment order for any employee and you post all your payroll liabilities to a single payroll liabilities account, don't include the garnishment in that posting; instead, create a specific payroll liability account for garnishments or you'll drive yourself crazy tracking the remittances. If you use specific payroll liability accounts for each type of liability (which I suggest), add an account for garnishments.

Payroll Expenses

Payroll expenses are the payments due from the employer. Like liabilities connected to the withholding from paychecks, most of the expenses are sent to government agencies, and they vary depending on the state and local jurisdiction in which you do business. Employer expenses can also include non-government expenses, depending on the benefits you provide. Employer expenses commonly include the following:

- Matching payments for the social security withheld from paychecks.

- Matching payments for the medicare withheld from paychecks.

- Federal unemployment tax (FUTA)

- State unemployment employer's tax (if applicable)

- State disability employer's tax (if applicable)

- Local employer tax (if applicable).

- Employer's contribution to benefits (if applicable).

- Workers' compensation insurance (if applicable).

NOTE: Employer payroll expenses are also called payroll *burden*.

Payroll Expenses are Really Liabilities

Because payroll expenses are required expenses, and are tied to the payroll, they're really payroll liabilities. You post these amounts as liabilities, but they end up as expenses, as you'll see in the following sections as I explain how your payroll is posted to the general ledger.

Posting Payroll Liabilities

Payroll liabilities are posted to payroll liability accounts, which are Other Current Liabilities. Some businesses post all liabilities to a single account named Payroll Liabilities. Other businesses post each liability to its own account (see Figure 9-1).

◇2010 · FIT WITHHELD	Other Current Liability
◇2020 · FICA WITHHELD	Other Current Liability
◇2030 · MEDICARE WITHHELD	Other Current Liability
◇2040 · PA INCOME TAX WITHHELD	Other Current Liability
◇2050 · PHILA WAGE TAX WITHHELD	Other Current Liability
◇2060 · EMPLOYEE U.C WITHHELD	Other Current Liability
◇2080 · MEDICAL BENEFITS W/H	Other Current Liability
◇2110 · Employer FICA Due	Other Current Liability
◇2120 · Employer Medicare Due	Other Current Liability
◇2130 · Employer FUTA Due	Other Current Liability
◇2140 · Employer SUTA Due	Other Current Liability
◇2200 · ACCRUED PENSION-ACCT 44578164	Other Current Liability

Figure 9-1: This chart of accounts tracks specific payroll liabilities.

If you do your own payroll, the liabilities are posted by your payroll software as you create the paychecks. If you have a payroll service, you use the report from the payroll service to post the liabilities by creating a journal entry. Table 9-2 represents the postings for the paychecks.

Account	Debit	Credit
Salaries & Wages	Total Salaries and Wages	
Fed Withholding Liability Account		Total Withheld
Social Security (FICA) Liability Account		Total Withheld
Medicare Liability Account		Total Withheld

Account	Debit	Credit
State Income Tax Liability Account		Total Withheld
Local Income Tax Liability Account		Total Withheld
State Disability Liability Account		Total Withheld
State SUI Liability Account		Total Withheld
Benefits Contrib Liability Account		Total Withheld
401(k) Contrib Liability Account		Total Withheld
Bank Account		Total Net Pay

Table 9-2: The total of withholdings and the net pay equals the total expense posted for salaries and wages.

In addition, payroll software and payroll service companies post the employer liabilities, using the payroll expense account as the other side of the ledger. Table 9-3 is an example of employer postings.

Debit	Credit
FICA Expense	Employer FICA Due Liability Account
Medicare Expense	Employer Medicare Due Liability Account
FUTA expense	Employer FUTA Due Liability Account
Benefits Expense	Employer Benefits Due Liability Account
Pension Expense	Employer 401(k) Due Liability Account

Table 9-3: Postings for employer payroll liabilities and expenses.

Posting Payroll Liability Payments

When you remit the payments to government agencies, insurance companies, pension plans, and so on, the postings "wash" (zero out) the amounts in the liability accounts. If you have a payroll service that remits your payments, you enter those transactions as a journal entry. Table 9-4 shows the postings for remitting a federal liability payment.

Account	Debit	Credit
Bank Account		3824.00
FIT Withheld	2600.00	
Employer FICA Due	496.00	
FICA Withheld	496.00	
Employer Medicare Due	116.00	
Medicare Withheld	116.00	

Table 9-4: Postings for remittance of federal payroll liabilities.

The same posting pattern occurs when you remit checks to other government agencies, and to non-government vendors. You post to the liability accounts and those postings remove ("wash") the liabilities.

Note that both the employee (withholding) and employer (expense) liabilities are "washed", but nothing touches the postings you made to the employer expenses. Those expenses remain and appear on your Profit & Loss report and are deductions on your tax return.

Independent Contractors

Posting payments to independent contractors isn't complicated; most of the time you post the checks to an expense account named Subcontractors or Outside Services. However, for those independent contractors who receive Form 1099, you have make sure you have the information you need to create and send the 1099s. This means you have to set up your accounting components properly and post payments to match your 1099 setup.

Who Gets Form 1099?

Most independent contractors that earn money from your business need to receive a 1099. The IRS has a very long list of Yes and No categories for the types of businesses that receive 1099s. In addition, there are multiple 1099 Forms for a variety of types of income.

Rather than fill a lot of space in this book with all the 1099 forms, I'll deal with the most common form that businesses send to independent contractors: Form 1099-MISC. In fact, most businesses (large, small and in-between) only need to prepare Form 1099-MISC.

Form 1099-MISC has multiple uses; there are boxes on the form for rents, royalties, and other income sources. For reporting payments to independent contractors, the applicable box is Box 7 – Nonemployee Compensation. A 1099 is required for Box 7 when the minimum amount earned is $600.00 (the minimum amount is called the *threshold*).

Following is a brief overview of the guidelines for Form 1099-MISC Box 7, although there are some exceptions to the broad statements I make here and you must check with your accountant when you're ready to create the 1099.

You must send a 1099-MISC to any individual or business that is not a corporation that you paid during the calendar year. Among the common types of transactions requiring you to send a 1099-MISC for Box 7 are:

- Payment for services, including payment for parts or materials used to perform the services if supplying the parts or materials was incidental to providing the service.

- Professional fees, such as fees to attorneys, accountants, architects, contractors, engineers, etc.

- Fees paid by one professional to another, such as fee-splitting or referral fees.

Configure Components for 1099s

To create 1099s you need to know which vendors get 1099s, and which posting accounts are included in determining the total payments for the 1099. Most accounting software has a setup routine that automates 1099 functions, but you have to be careful about accuracy when you go through the 1099 setup program (reading the Help files makes this task easier and more accurate than "guessing").

If you're not using accounting software, create a method for identifying vendors who receive 1099s. If you use Excel, create another column named 1099 and enter data (an "X" or a "Y") for the appropriate vendors. Do the same thing for the expense accounts in your chart of accounts; create a method of determining which expense accounts are used to record payments to independent contractors who must receive Form 1099. When you're ready to prepare 1099s re-sort the worksheets by the 1099 column to display all the appropriate data contiguously.

To create a list of 1099 recipients, the following formula controls the data: **Vendors enabled for 1099 who have received payments posted to the 1099-enabled accounts are 1099 recipients**.

- Vendors who are not 1099-enabled who received payments posted to 1099-enabled accounts don't appear in the list.

- Vendors who are 1099-enabled who received some payments posted to 1099-enabled accounts and some payments posted to accounts that are not 1099-enabled, appear on the list and the total amount reportable includes only payments made to 1099-enabled accounts.

- Vendors who are 1099-enabled who received all their payments posted to accounts that are not 1099-enabled don't appear in the list. (This is highly improbable and probably means you didn't set up your accounts properly for 1099 reporting.)

You must have the vendor's business name (which may be the vendor's own name), the correct address, and the Tax Identification Number (TIN). The tax identification number is either a Social Security Number (for individuals) or an Employer Identification Number (EIN) for a business.

All independent contractors, consultants, and other self-employed workers who perform work for you should fill out Form W-9–Request for Taxpayer Identification Number and Certification. This form provides you with the information you need to create Form 1099.

TIP: I suggest that you have a policy of not issuing an independent contractor their first payment until they have given you Form W-9.

You don't send Form W-9 to the IRS; you keep it in your files. You can get Form W-9 from the IRS by entering the following URL into your browser's Address Bar: **http://www.**

irs.gov/pub/irs-pdf/fw9.pdf). When the file opens, use the Print command on your browser to print as many copies as you need.

Reimbursing Independent Contractors for Expenses

If a vendor purchases something for your business as part of the job, it's normal to include reimbursable expenses in the check you send without separating out those expenses. You post the entire check to Outside Services (or whatever you've named the expense account for paying independent contractors). The independent contractor tracks the total amount of the check as income, and indicates the expenses in his or her own tax return.

However, some businesses and some independent contractors prefer to treat out-of-pocket outlays for the business as expenses to the business that should be reimbursed separately from payments for work.

If you adopt this approach for an independent contractor, posting the payment is slightly different because the expense is your expense rather than the vendor's expense. When you pay the contractor create a split transaction. As seen in Table 9-5, post the reimbursed expense to the applicable expense account in your chart of accounts and post the payment for work to the expense you use for outside services.

Account	Debit	Credit
6400 – Outside Services	5000.00	
6150 – Office Supplies	250.00	
1000 – Bank account		5250.00

Table 9-5: You can split a payment to an independent contractor to separate reimbursements from payments for work.

You have to be sure that the expense account you use in this situation is not linked to your 1099 configuration. That way, the amount posted for services is carried to the 1099, but the amount for reimbursement is not.

Chapter 10

Year End Tasks

At the end of your fiscal year (usually the same as the calendar year for small businesses) you have to perform a number of tasks to make sure your financial information is ready for tax preparation and to prepare your books for your next fiscal year.

In this chapter I discuss the common year-end tasks you face, and also explain the various tax forms you have to think about as you prepare reports on your finances.

Depreciation and Amortization

Depreciation and amortization are expenses you deduct against the costs of major purchases that have been recorded as assets. Depreciation is for tangible assets (things you can see and touch such as equipment, furniture, etc.) and amortization is for intangible assets (such as patents, the organizational costs of starting a business, etc.).

Theoretically, you calculate the yearly expense/deduction by dividing the cost of the asset by the number of years the asset is expected to last or be useful. I use the word "theoretically" because it doesn't really work in a straightforward manner. First of all, some assets are hard to define in terms of useful life; you often can't predict with any confidence their rate of "wear and tear" or "obsolescence". Secondly, IRS rules, state laws, and court decisions have introduced many exceptions to the way depreciation and amortization amounts can be calculated.

The reason we have depreciation and amortization deductions is that when you spend money on a major purchase for something that will be used for a period of years, you're usually not allowed to deduct the total expense of the purchase the year you purchase it. If you'd declared the total cost as an expense you'd have an understatement of your company's profit that year, and an overstatement of profit in the following years. Since the asset is being used to operate the company for multiple years, that's not good accounting.

Creating a Depreciation/Amortization Transaction

The transaction you create to record depreciation and/or amortization is different from most transactions in two ways:

- Unlike most transactions (such as selling a product or buying goods or services), no money is involved. You don't write a check and you don't deposit funds in the bank.

- Because of the complicated regulations for these deductions, the amount of the transaction is not easy to calculate; instead you should ask your accountant for guidance.

(Some businesses use one set of depreciation rules for keeping their books and another, more aggressive set of depreciation entries, for reporting their taxes – this definitely requires input from your accountant.)

The transaction for depreciation/amortization is a journal entry, reducing the value of the asset (a credit posted to the contra-asset account) and increasing expenses (a debit posted to the depreciation and/or amortization expense account). In effect, you're recognizing the wear and tear, obsolescence, or other decline in value of the asset by reducing its value and taking a tax deduction against that loss in value. Table 10-1 is a typical journal entry for depreciation; a journal entry for amortization takes the same form, using the appropriate accounts.

Account	Debit	Credit
1710 – Accum Deprec-Furniture & Fixtures		450.00
1720 – Accum Deprec-Vehicles		600.00
1730 – Accum Deprec-Equipment		550.00
6600 – Depreciation Expense	1600.00	

Table 10-1: Depreciation and amortization are posted with a journal entry.

The journal entry displayed here uses asset accounts specifically created for the purpose of posting accumulated depreciation for each type of fixed asset. A separate asset account exists for posting the original purchases for each category (Furniture & Fixtures, Vehicles, Equipment, etc.).

Some businesses have only a single account for each asset category, instead of using separate accounts for cost and accumulated depreciation. When depreciation is posted, the single asset account balance is reduced. A more detailed discussion of the choices for managing fixed asset accounts and depreciation is in Chapter 11.

Fixed Asset Dispositions

Fixed asset dispositions occur when you sell a fixed asset or you stop using it because it's no longer useful (called *retiring the asset*). In either case, you need to remove the original cost and the accumulated depreciation associated with the asset from your books. To accomplish this, the amount of depreciation that was recorded against the fixed asset is added back, and the original cost of the fixed asset is removed.

If you don't remove the fixed asset when you dispose of it, your Balance Sheet report shows the original costs and depreciation, inherently stating that the asset still exists. This can cause confusion when a lender, potential investor, or potential buyer relies on the assets included in your Balance Sheet. It can also cause a problem when an insurance agent tries to reconcile a listing of the assets included in your books with those included on your insurance policies.

Sale of Fixed Assets

When you sell a fixed asset, in addition to removing the original cost and the depreciation that was taken, you have to post the income you received from the buyer of the fixed asset. To remove the fixed asset and record the proceeds of the sale, your accountant makes the following journal entry:

1.   Records any depreciation allowed for the final year of ownership.

2.   Adds back all the depreciation taken over the years (including the final year, if any depreciation was recorded in Step 1).

3.   Reverses the original cost of the fixed asset.

4.   Records the bank deposit for the payment you received from the buyer.

At this point, the journal entry doesn't balance; the difference is the net gain or loss on the sale of the asset (which is not necessarily the amount you received from the buyer).

Let's use a real example so you can follow the money.

- You purchased a fixed asset (a piece of equipment, a car, etc.) for $10,000.00. You recorded the purchase with a debit to the appropriate Fixed Assets account.

- Over the years, you took $7000.00 of depreciation. Each year, the depreciation was a credit to the asset account named Accumulated Depreciation and a debit to an expense account named Depreciation (the expense reduced your taxable profit each year).

- Now you've sold the asset for $2400.00 and deposited the buyer's check in your bank account (a debit to the bank account).

Table 10-2 shows the postings for these amounts, but this is not yet a transaction because the debit and credit columns aren't equal. (Note that the postings for Accumulated Depreciation and Fixed Assets are the opposite of the original postings made when you purchased the asset and when depreciation was taken each year.)

Account	Debit	Credit
Accumulated Depreciation	7000.00	
Fixed Assets		10000.00
Bank Account	2400.00	
Totals	9400.00	10000.00

Table 10-2: This entry doesn't balance; the difference is the net gain or loss on the sale of the asset.

In this case, we need to add $600.00 to the Debit side of the entry to balance the transaction. The posting is usually to an Income account named Gain on Sale of Fixed Assets. Income is a credit, but in this case the posting is a debit. This means the amount is "contra-income", which is the same as an expense. You actually have a net loss of $600.00 for the fixed asset, which reduces your taxable income.

Of course, before your accountant creates this entry you want to deposit the buyer's check in your bank account, and that means you have to post it in your accounting records. I suggest you create an account specifically for the purpose of recording this sale. Add an Other Income account named Proceeds of Fixed Asset Sales to your chart of accounts and use it when you post the deposit. Isolating this transaction in this account highlights the sale so your accountant can identify it. Your accountant creates the entries required to remove the asset from your books, record the profit or loss from the sale of the fixed asset, and adjust the entry you made to this "temporary" account.

Retirement of Fixed Assets

Fixed assets retirements occur when an asset is no longer in use. A common example is a computer that became obsolete and is sitting in a closet or has been thrown away.

Since a fixed asset that is being retired has already been completely depreciated, the cost of the fixed asset is the same as its accumulated depreciation. The combination of these amounts results in a zero balance carried on your books for the fixed asset, but the individual account balances (the debit posting for the original cost and the credit postings for accumulated depreciation) are still appearing on your Balance Sheet report. Your accountant removes those individual balances from your books by posting a credit to the original purchase account and a debit to the accumulated depreciation account (the opposite of the original postings).

Adjustments for Cash Basis Tax Reports

You'll find a complete discussion about the difference between accrual and cash based accounting in Chapter 1. For this discussion on year-end tasks I'll assume you keep your books on accrual basis (a better way to get a handle on the financial health of your business), but you file your taxes on cash basis.

To get the figures you need for your cash-based tax return you have to remove the A/R and A/P totals that appear on your balance sheet. Performing this task requires two journal entries; first you remove the A/R and A/P totals (to match your books with your tax return), then you put them back (to continue tracking your company's financials with details about A/R and A/P). This special type of journal entry is called a *reversing journal entry*. The original journal entry is posted on a given date, and is reversed on a later date.

The original journal entry you create for cash basis tax reports is dated the last day of the year and the reversing journal entry is posted the next day. That way, when you look at your year-end report, your accounting records match the tax return.

Table 10-3 represents a journal entry on the last day of the year to remove A/P (vendor bills recorded but not yet paid), using an expense account created specifically for this purpose.

Date	Account	Debit	Credit
12/31	2100 – Accounts Payable	1200.00	
12/31	9999 – Adjustment for Cash Basis		1200.00

Table 10-3: Decrease A/P and expenses to remove accrued amounts from your balance sheet and Profit & Loss report.

To remove A/R totals (invoices sent to customers that are not yet paid), the process is the same. You can use the same adjustment account you created for adjusting A/P, or create an income adjustment account. The net result on the Profit & Loss statement is the same either way, but some business owners and accountants prefer the clarity of a separate account for the A/R journal entry.)

For A/R, the postings are as follows:

- Credit A/R.
- Debit the offset account.

You could also do both adjustments at once in a single journal entry (which is the way many accountants perform this task) as seen in Table 10-4.

Date	Account	Debit	Credit
12/31	2100 – Accounts Payable	1200.00	
12/31	1100 – Accounts Receivable		1600.00
12/31	9999 – Adjustment for Cash Basis	400.00	

Table 10-4: You can make all your cash-basis adjustments in one J/E.

Arithmetically, these "summary" J/Es accomplish the purpose. However, some people prefer to be more precise by noting the specific accounts that are affected by the adjustments. For example, to adjust A/P you debit the A/P account and then individually credit each expense account for which an open vendor bill exists. This requires some research, but if you are extremely fussy about details and precision (and some accountants are) you can create the longer J/E.

These journal entries assume that all your unpaid vendor bills are linked to expense accounts and all your unpaid customer invoices are linked to income accounts. However, that's not always the case. Some of the unpaid bills in the A/P total may be linked to liability accounts, such as bank loan payments. Some of the unpaid invoices in the A/R total may be invoices for retainers or upfront deposits (both of which are liabilities). If that's the case, the journal entry should include postings to the appropriate liability and asset accounts in addition to the expense and income accounts linked to the A/P and A/R totals. For the income and expense postings you can use a generic adjustment account.

Allocating Overhead Expenses to Divisions

If you're tracking divisions with software that provides a divisionalized chart of accounts, you can allocate overhead expenses to those divisions at year-end. This gives you a more precise Profit & Loss report for each division. (Chapter 2 has information about setting up and using a divisionalized chart of accounts.)

The specific expenses incurred by each division were posted to that division's expenses as you paid them, but there are always some overhead expenses that are company-wide and can be allocated across the divisions. Usually allocation is either calculated to each division evenly, or you allocate a percentage of the expense to each division. If you allocate by percentage, you need a formula, which can be based on the size of the division (such as number of employees, or the total of specific expenses, or the total of income). Some expenses are easier to calculate; such as automobile insurance, which is allocated depending on the number of vehicles used by each division.

Allocation is effected by a journal entry that removes an amount from the top level (company wide) expense account and posts it to the same expense account for the division, as seen in Table 10-5.

Account	Debit	Credit
6450-6450-00 – Insurance-Vehicles		4200.00
6450-6450-01 – Insurance-Vehicles	1800.00	
6450-6450-02 – Insurance-Vehicles	2400.00	

Table 10-5: Allocate expenses to divisions to get a more realistic Profit & Loss report for each division.

Allocating Equity

Companies that have multiple owners need to allocate the company's profit or loss among the owners at the end of the year. (A proprietorship, a single member LLC, or an S Corporation with only one stockholder obviously doesn't have to worry about this.) The allocated amount appears on the tax form provided to each owner/partner.

NOTE: Regardless of the number of stockholders, C corporations don't allocate equity because the profits aren't passed to the stockholders' tax returns. A C corporation files a tax return for the business and pays its own taxes.

For an S Corporation with more than one owner, the distribution must be made in the same percentage as the stock ownership of each stockholder. An owner of 50% of the stock is allocated 50% of the profits, a 10% stockholder gets 10% of the profits, and so on.

For a partnership, an LLP, or a multimember LLC, the operating agreement created by the owners sets the allocation percentage (these agreements don't always use the amount of capital contributed as the allocation basis).

Some accounting software programs perform this task for you, offering equity accounts for allocation during the year-end closing process. Be sure to check the numbers with your accountant before entering them. If you use accounting software that doesn't offer an equity allocation procedure, accounting software that doesn't have a year-end closing process, or if you don't use accounting software, your accountant creates the necessary transactions as part of the year-end procedures.

In addition to allocating the profit/loss to multiple owners, your accountant may choose to consolidate each owner's financial data into a single account, and the total in that account becomes the opening balance for each owner/partner in the new year. This task is only performed if you maintain separate accounts for capital contributions and draw for each owner/partner. To accomplish this, your accountant takes the totals of each individual account and merges them so the new single account holds the net amount (capital less draw).

For all types of businesses (single owner or multiple owners), some accounting software rolls the current year's profit/loss into an historical retained earnings account and starts the new year with a zero balance in the profit/loss account. For software that doesn't offer this process, some accountants choose to perform this task manually, while other accountants prefer to let retained earnings continue to roll forward into the new year.

Tax Forms and Tax Returns

Your business may have to produce tax forms and/or tax returns. Tax forms are those forms you provide to employees and independent contractors. A tax return is the method by which you report your business earnings and pay taxes on the profits. Some businesses file tax returns that stand on their own. Others file forms reporting the business activities as part of the owners' personal tax returns.

Tax Forms

At the end of the year, your company may have to produce some tax forms, specifically Form W-2 if you have employees, and Form 1099 if you pay independent contractors. (Information about tracking payroll and independent contractors is in Chapter 9.)

You can file these forms on paper or electronically. If you have 250 or more forms to file you must file electronically. In this section I'll go over these tax forms, and in the sections following I'll discuss business tax returns.

W-2

Every employee must receive Form W-2. Employees attach the W-2 to their personal tax returns, and you file copies with the Social Security Administration, your state revenue department and any other tax entity that requires a copy (e.g. a local tax authority). You also keep a copy for your files.

When you send the forms to the Social Security Administration you must include Form W-3 – Transmittal of Wage and Tax Statements. This is a summary form that indicates the number of W-2s you are filing and the totals for each box on the W-2s you issued.

If you have an outside payroll service, the service produces the W-2s and sends them to the appropriate recipients. If you do payroll in-house, you must prepare the W-2s. You buy the forms (at any office supply store) and your software produces the reports. If you do in-house payroll manually, you can buy the forms with software that sends the forms to a printer. You can also file W-2s and W-3s electronically. Learn more about this service by visiting the SSA website at **http://www.socialsecurity.gov/employer/**.

1099

You must issue Form 1099 to every independent contractor who qualifies for the form (see Chapter 9 for more information on tracking payments to independent contractors). You can create the forms from your accounting software, or from software designed for this purpose. In fact, you can buy packages of 1099 forms with software enclosed in the package at any office supply store.

Send the forms to the IRS, along with Form 1096 - Annual Summary and Transmittal of U.S. Information Returns. (Form 1096 contains the total amount reported from all forms being submitted.)

NOTE: Some states and localities require that you file copies of 1099s you prepare.

Business Tax Returns

Business owners have to file tax returns that include the profit/loss of their businesses. However, not all businesses file tax returns in the business name; some forms of businesses report taxable income on the personal tax returns of the owners or members. In this section I'll provide a brief overview of the tax return methods used by each type of business entity.

Proprietorship Tax Return

Proprietorships don't file a federal or state income tax return. Instead, the profit of the business is reported, and the tax paid, on the owner's personal tax returns.

For federal tax returns, the profit is reported on Schedule C and the net profit/loss amount on Schedule C is included on Form 1040. The owner pays the income taxes personally (along with self employment taxes as a way of being included in the social security system).

Any state and local tax returns are handled in the same fashion, with the owner remitting taxes based on the profit of the business as reported on Schedule C.

It's important to note that the amount included for income tax reporting purposes is the calculated profit of the business, not the draw taken by the owner during the year.

Single Member LLC Tax Return

A single member LLC isn't recognized as an independent entity by the IRS, and federal tax returns are prepared and filed as if the business were a proprietorship. This means that just like a proprietorship, the single member files Schedule C and reports the profit on Form 1040. State and local tax returns are also based on the profit of the business, not the amount the owner withdrew.

NOTE: There is no limitation to the number of proprietorships or single member LLCs that can be included on an individual federal tax return. Each business requires its own Schedule C. The amount reported on page 1 of Form 1040 is the sum of all Schedule Cs included with the tax return.

Partnership Tax Return

At the end of the year, a partnership prepares and files its own federal tax return (Form 1065) but pays no income taxes on its own behalf. The partners are responsible for paying the taxes due on their shares of the business' income on their personal tax returns. The information recorded in Form 1065 comes from the partnership's Profit & Loss statement as well as its Balance Sheet (both of which are discussed in Chapter 11).

Each partner receives Schedule K-1, which reports his or her share of the profits. (You can think of this as similar to a W-2.) Each partner's share of the profits is based on the profit and loss report, and not the amount of the partner's draw. If the profit is larger than the draw, the amount of the profit is treated as if the partner had drawn all profits and then contributed the amount not drawn back to the partnership to fund its continuing operations. These funds are available for withdrawal by the partner at a later time with no additional income tax consequences.

If applicable, Schedule K-1 also reports other transactions specific to that partner (covered in Chapter 7):

- Interest and dividend income
- Health insurance premiums.
- Retirement plan contributions.
- State income tax payments for partners who are not residents of the state in which the partnership does business (and the partner can take credit for those payments on his or her personal return).

Each partner reports the net profit reported on the Schedule K-1 on his or her personal tax return, using Schedule E. The other income and payments from the partnership that appear on

Schedule K-1 are also reported on Form 1040, but not normally on Schedule E.

Your state may require partnerships to file a tax return, and some states collect income taxes from the partners as well as business taxes and/or fees imposed on the partnership. These funds are remitted with the partnership return you file with the state.

State business fees are deductible as a business expense by the partnership. Income taxes that are paid by the partnership for the benefit of the partners are not deductible expenses for the partnership; instead they are treated a draw. Some states only require estimated income tax payments for nonresident partners. Nonresident partners file income tax returns in any nonresident states they have reportable income (receiving credit for the estimated nonresident state taxes paid on their behalf). When these partners file state income tax returns in their home state they receive credit for taxes paid to any other state).

When you remit business tax returns and payments to the state, you post the partners' tax payments to each partner's draw accounts. Regular business fees owed to the state by the partnership are business expenses. Table 10-6 represents the postings for state business taxes as well as nonresident state income tax payments made for the benefit of nonresident partners B and C (partner A is a resident of the state).

Account	Debit	Credit
3602 – Draw-Partner B-State Tax	300.00	
3603 – Draw- Partner C-State Tax	200.00	
8500 – Business Taxes and Licenses	100.00	
1000 – Bank Account		600.00

Table 10-6: Only state taxes imposed on the partnership are business expenses.

LLP or Multimember LLC Tax Return

The returns and procedures for LLPs and Multimember LLCs are the same as for partnerships for both federal and state taxes. The business files Form 1065, but pays no federal business taxes. Any taxes paid are personal taxes for the partners/members and are based on the information on Form K-1 (see the discussion on partnership returns earlier in this section).

The IRS treats a multimember LLC as a partnership by default. However, a multimember LLC can elect to be treated as a corporation, including an S corporation, by filing Form 8832 – Entity Classification Election. This isn't a common action, but if your company has elected to be treated as a corporation the information in the following sections for corporate tax returns applies.

S Corporation Tax Return

An S Corporation tax return is similar to that of a partnership (S corps are hybrid organizations, mixing some corporate conventions with partnership conventions). The corporation files a tax return (Form 1120S) but usually pays no income taxes on its own behalf. Included with the return is Schedule K-1, which reports the profit for each stockholder and a summary of any other transactions specific to that stockholder. (Many S corporations have a single stockholder.)

As with partnerships, LLPs, and multimember LLCs, a stockholder's share of the profits is based on the profit and loss report and not the amount of the stockholder's draw. To the extent the profit is larger than the draw you can look at it as if the stockholder had drawn all of his/her profit share out and then contributed the amount not drawn out back to the business to fund its continuing operations; the funds should be available for withdrawal at a later time with no income tax consequence.

The stockholder reports the net profit on Schedule E of his or her personal tax return. Other financial transactions reported on Schedule K-1 are reported on the stockholder's tax forms the same as if they had been received from, or paid by, a sole proprietor.

The S Corporation also files state income tax returns for every state in which it conducts business. As with partnerships, LLPs and multimember LLCs, most states impose state income tax for each stockholder who is not resident in that state. The amount of the tax is based on the stockholder's share of the business profit. These payments to the state are often made by the S Corporation, but are not a business expense; instead they are posted as a draw for those stockholders. Nonresident stockholders can take credit for these payments on their personal tax returns.

C Corporation Tax Return

A C Corporation files federal Form 1120 and applicable state corporate tax returns. The corporation pays taxes on the corporation's profits.

Stockholders may receive other tax forms, depending on the situation: W-2 for wages, 1099-MISC for directors' fees, 1099-INT for interest, and 1099-DIV for dividends. The amounts on these forms are reported on the stockholder's personal tax returns the same as they would be if they were received from any other entity.

Chapter 11

Important Reports

• •

Business owners should examine financial reports frequently, because the reports provide a "health" report on your business. It's important to understand what data is in each type of report, and what the data means. Accountants constantly receive questions from clients who don't understand why certain accounts aren't listed on certain reports, or why accounts that appear on the reports have balances they don't understand. I've gathered a list of some of the most common questions of this type and I'll include answers to those questions as I explain the important financial reports you should be keeping an eye on.

Balance Sheet

The balance sheet is a snapshot of your financial position at a particular moment in time. By "particular moment in time" I mean the date you choose when you create the report, which could be the current date, or the last day of the previous year, quarter, or month.

NOTE: Another term for balance sheet is *statement of financial position.*

The balance sheet is the primary "health record" for your business. It shows what your business owns, what it owes to others, and its equity (a combination of owners/stockholders investments and the company's profit/loss). The balance sheet has two traits you have to be aware of:

- The word "balance" means the numbers must balance using the formula **assets = liabilities + equity**.

- The totals in the balance sheet reflect the entire life of your business, the numbers roll on from year to year; they don't start fresh each year. Each account displays the "net balance" of all activity in that account since Day One.

Because the balance sheet has such important information about your company's financial health, it's usually the report that bankers want to see first when you apply for a loan. Investors (or potential investors) also typically start their investigations by looking at the balance sheet. For public corporations that have to make financial reports available to stockholders, the balance sheet is the first report investors want to see because the value of their ownership is reflected in the equity section of this report.

Balance Sheet Assets

What your business owns is displayed in the Assets section of your balance sheet, and Figure 11-1 shows that portion of a balance sheet.

Some of the accounts in the assets section of the balance sheet raise questions in the minds of business owners, and this is a good place to go over some of the most common questions that accountants receive.

ASSETS
- **Current Assets**
  - **Checking/Savings**

1000 · Operating Account	66,108.35
1030 · Money Market Accnt	5,409.25
1050 · Payroll Account	1,999.00
1060 · Petty Cash	1,230.00
Total Checking/Savings	74,746.60
Accounts Receivable	
1200 · Accounts Receivable	36,750.42
Total Accounts Receivable	36,750.42
Other Current Assets	
1100 · Inventory Asset	2,657.60
1505 · Purchase Prepayments	1,000.00
Total Other Current Assets	3,657.60
Total Current Assets	115,154.62
Fixed Assets	
1600 · Equipment	
1601 · Equipment Purchases	3,412.00
1602 · Accum Deprec-Equipment	-2,250.00
Total 1600 · Equipment	1,162.00
1610 · Furn & Fixtures	
1611 · Purchases-Furn & Fixtures	6,550.32
1612 · Accum Depr-Furn & Fixtures	-2,800.00
Total 1610 · Furn & Fixtures	3,750.32
1620 · Vehicles	
1621 · Vehicles-Purchases	5,000.00
1622 · Accum Depr-Vehicles	-2,100.00
Total 1620 · Vehicles	2,900.00
Total Fixed Assets	7,812.32
TOTAL ASSETS	**122,966.94**

Figure 11-1: The assets represent what your business owns.

Balance Sheet Bank Accounts

The balance sheet shows the bank balances in your bank registers as of the date of the balance sheet. Usually, the balance sheet is created for the last day of a year, quarter, or month.

If you have a copy of your bank statement for the same period, the bank's balance almost certainly is different from the balance on your balance sheet report. Many business owners call their accountants to get an explanation for the fact that their balance sheet amount and the closing amount on the bank's statement don't match.

Your bank register balance reflects all the activity in the bank account, every check you wrote and every deposit you entered. The bank statement reflects all the transactions you created that have cleared the bank. It does not include checks that haven't yet been deposited by the payees, and it does not reflect deposits you made that didn't clear the bank in time for the statement (usually these are deposits made on the last or next-to-last day before the statement closing date, or credit card payments that your merchant account doesn't deposit for a few days).

Eventually those checks and deposits that weren't included in the bank's closing balance clear, but the bank's balance still won't "catch up" in the next statement, because you'll have written more checks and made more deposits that didn't clear before you get the next statement.

Balance Sheet Fixed Assets Accounts

The sample balance sheet displays the fixed assets, at their original cost, in a detailed manner. The purchase of fixed assets is posted to its own account (fixed asset-purchases, or fixed asset-cost), and the depreciation is posted separately to its own contra-account (accumulated depreciation-fixed asset).

The balance sheet displays both posting totals and reports the current net value of the fixed assets. The history of the individual fixed assets within a category is usually kept in a separate schedule in order to keep the balance sheet presentation clean.

Some accountants and business owners prefer to consolidate the cost and accumulated depreciation into a single account for each type of fixed asset. In that case the balance sheet displays the net value (cost less accumulated depreciation) in its fixed assets section.

If your fixed assets are posted to a single account for each category, and the value of each category changes from year to year, it's because purchases, dispositions, and depreciation are posted to that single account and are included in the total you see. (Dispositions are assets that have either been sold or scrapped because they are no longer usable. Because the balance sheet assets include only things you own, ask your accountant how to remove these assets from your books.)

If you use a single account instead of separate accounts for purchases and depreciation, the displayed total is the current net value. The arithmetic is the same no matter how you set up your chart of accounts for fixed assets; the difference is only in the details that are displayed in the report.

Balance Sheet Other Assets Accounts

The balance sheet sample for the company I displayed in this chapter did not have any other asset accounts. That is not unusual for many small businesses. While fixed assets are tangible (you can touch them), you may have other assets that are intangible and have value that will last for more than one year.

Record these intangible assets similarly to the way you record fixed assets. It's best to have one account listing the original cost and a separate account (a contra account) listing the accumulated amortization. Amortization is the term for the periodic writing down of intangible assets, and it's the same process as applying depreciation to fixed assets. (Amortization is covered in Chapter 10.)

These other assets are normally displayed below the fixed assets in the balance sheet, just before the total for all assets owned. Common other assets are:

- Start Up Costs
- Goodwill
- Copyrights and Patents

NOTE: The value of fixed assets and intangible assets on the balance sheet are the results of tracking your transactions, including the original cost and the accumulated depreciation/amortization. These figures are not related to current market value.

Balance Sheet Liabilities and Equity

The section of the balance sheet that displays liabilities and equity looks similar to Figure 11-2. Notice that the total at the bottom matches the total for assets.

Some of the categories and accounts in this section of the balance sheet can also cause confusion, so in this section I'll go over some of the most common questions accounts receive.

Balance Sheet Sales Tax Liability Account

Sales tax liabilities cause questions from business owners, and also cause problems in accounting data files that accountants have to clean up (and sometimes the cleanup isn't a cakewalk). In terms of the process, tracking sales tax is very logical.

1. When you collect sales tax you post the sales tax amount to a liability account (usually named Sales Tax Payable). Posting sales tax collected in sales transactions is covered in Chapter 3.

2. When you remit sales tax you post the payment to the same liability account to reduce the balance. Remitting sales tax is covered in Chapter 6.

LIABILITIES & EQUITY	
Liabilities	
Current Liabilities	
Accounts Payable	
2000 · **Accounts Payable**	2,179.00
Total Accounts Payable	2,179.00
Credit Cards	
2050 · **Visa - MyBank**	3,271.00
Total Credit Cards	3,271.00
Other Current Liabilities	
2200 · **Sales Tax Payable**	3.00
Total Other Current Liabilities	3.00
Total Current Liabilities	5,453.00
Long Term Liabilities	
2700 · **Bank Loan #2252**	5,000.00
Total Long Term Liabilities	5,000.00
Total Liabilities	10,453.00
Equity	
3130 · **Owner's Capital**	
3140 · **Owner's Capital Contributions**	8,430.28
3150 · **Draws**	-2,800.00
3151 · **Personal payment of bus exp**	725.00
Total 3130 · Owner's Capital	6,355.28
3900 · **Retained Earnings**	97,547.97
Net Income	8,610.69
Total Equity	112,513.94
TOTAL LIABILITIES & EQUITY	**122,966.94**

Figure 11-2: Liabilities plus equity must equal assets.

If you remit sales tax monthly on the 10th day of the following month, the amount of sales tax displayed on your balance sheet on the 11th day of the month should be equal to the sales tax collected in the current month on days 1 through 11 (the balance left after you remit the previous month's tax).

However, many accountants find very large balances in the sales tax liability account (or business owners call to say the balance is way too large). How does this happen? Following are the two common reasons for this problem:

- You use accounting software that tracks sales tax and has a sales tax liability payment feature (almost all accounting software has this function). However, when you remit the sales tax you enter a check in the bank register instead of going through the payment feature. The liability account isn't "washed". Following the instructions in the Help files for using all the steps in the sales tax payment functions avoids this problem.

- You don't use software that tracks sales tax and when you have to remit sales tax you've collected you try to "figure out" where to post the payment. Many business owners incorrectly end up creating an expense account named Sales Tax (sales tax is not an expense nor is it income). The liability account isn't "washed". Post the remittance to the sales tax liability to avoid this problem.

Balance Sheet Loan Liability Accounts

A business sends a payment for a loan every month. Periodically, the bank sends a statement of the current loan balance. The bank's loan balance doesn't match the balance displayed on the balance sheet; the bank's loan balance is higher than the loan balance on your balance sheet. The business owner calls the accountant to get an explanation about the difference.

This happens when you post the entire loan payment to the loan liability account. Loans have interest, and the interest has to be posted separately from the payment to principal (interest is a deductible business expense and is posted to an expense account named Interest Expense). Instructions for creating transactions for loan payments are in Chapter 6.

Profit & Loss Report

The Profit & Loss report (nicknamed *the P & L*) is the report that most business owners rely on the most (and look at most often). This report displays all your income accounts and their balances, all your expense accounts and their balances, and your net profit (or loss). Like the balance sheet, the P & L has a formula: **Net Profit/Loss = Income – Expenses**.

NOTE: The Profit & Loss report is also called the *Income Statement* or the *Operating Statement*.

The terminology you see in a P & L reports varies according to the software you use. Some software uses the term Net Profit, other software uses the term Net Income. Some software inserts a minus sign to indicate a net loss; other software puts parentheses around the net amount if it's a loss.

Software also varies in the order in which totals and subtotals are displayed. Some software displays Other Income below the Ordinary Income total and displays Other Expenses below the Ordinary Expenses total. Other software displays Other Income/Expenses just above the net profit/loss figure, after displaying the Net Income/Loss figure calculated by adding ordinary income to ordinary expenses (as seen in Figure 11-3).

If your business tracks Cost of Goods Sold (COGS), those expenses are listed directly below the total income. The resulting net number (Income less COGS) is your *gross profit*. Usually, other operating expenses appear below the gross profit, and the net profit is the result of the formula: **Gross Profit less Operating Expenses**.

Income

	4010 Sales-Products	2,770.00
	4120 Sales-Service	16,740.00
	4040 · Reimbursed Exps	30.00
Total Income		**19,540.00**

Cost of Goods Sold

	5000 · Cost of Goods Sold	2,890.00
	5010 · Inventory Adjustments	-2,250.00
Total COGS		**640.00**
Gross Profit		**18,900.00**

Expense

	6030 · Medical Benefits	450.00
	6110 · Automobile Expense	99.42
	6150 · Depreciation Exp	7,150.00
	6170 · Equip Rental	25.00
	6290 · Rent	800.00
	6390 · Utilities	20.00
	6555 · Outside Services	1,850.00
Total Expense		**10,394.42**
Net Ordinary Income		**8,505.58**

Other Income

	7030 · Other Income	105.11
Total Other Income		**105.11**
Net Income		**8,610.69**

Figure 11-3: Your profit/loss is the last item in a P&L –
the "bottom line".

Net Profit or Loss

Business owners and accountants usually move their eyes
immediately to the bottom entry, the net profit/loss. Note that this
figure is the same as the Net Income figure in the Liabilities and
Equity section of the balance sheet (refer back to Figure 11-2).

Your net profit on the P & L is part of your company's
equity on the balance sheet when the two reports are created
to show the entire year (which is really year-to-date when you
create the report before the last day of the year). If you create a

P & L report for a specific period (such as a month, or a quarter) the P & L report profit/loss figure won't match the amount on the balance sheet report (which always displays year-to-date totals).

Unlike the balance sheet, which reflects the entire life of your business (the numbers roll over from year to year), the P & L report starts all over on the first day of your fiscal year. At the end of your fiscal year the amount of the net profit/loss is transferred to the balance sheet and all the income and expense accounts are zeroed out. As you create transactions that post to income and expense accounts, the P & L rebuilds itself for the current year. Accounting software does this automatically. If you're not using accounting software, start a new page or worksheet for each income and expense account for the new year.

Analyzing Your Business From the Profit & Loss Report

It's tempting to look at your P & L report and think, "I could increase my net profit if I increased my income and/or reduced my expenses". Unfortunately, it's not usually that simple.

You can increase your income by raising prices, or by increasing the size of your customer base. Raising prices is a high-risk decision because you could lose customers to your competition. If you lose enough customers, the higher prices result in less profit. The risk in increasing your customer base is that more customers and the higher volume of product sales also increase expenses, especially variable expenses.

There are different types of expenses and you have to do your analysis with an understanding of their meanings. Basically, there are two types of expenses in your P & L report: *Variable expenses* and *fixed expenses*.

Variable expenses are those expenses that are directly affected by (and linked to) sales. Providing products requires raw materials, labor, space, shipping, commissions, and other expenses. (These are the expenses that are usually posted to Cost of Goods Sold.) Selling one more widget means paying for all of the costs to get one more widget on your shelf.

Fixed expenses are the expenses that are fairly consistent because they don't vary widely as a result of a change in sales figures. These are the fundamental overhead costs such as insurance, rent, utilities, etc. Fixed expenses are sometimes listed in the P & L report as General and Administrative Costs.

Some experts add a third category of expenses, called *discretionary expenses*, which include wages, benefits, and other expenses that may be administrative, but can be changed to meet the needs of the company.

Many management consultants and small business experts warn that one of the largest causes of failure for small business is the inability to manage growth. These businesses expand their customer base or product line (or both), and then don't have sufficient resources to handle the growth. Original customers don't get the attention they're used to and new customers don't get the attention they expect unless more employees are brought onboard. If there isn't sufficient capital to add employees, the customers start shopping elsewhere. The widgets you need to have on hand to sell to those new customers require capital, because usually you have to pay your vendor before your new customers pay you. Many businesses can't recover economically from the increased costs of producing more goods if the time period before those goods are sold is lengthy.

Accounts Receivable Report

The A/R report shows you how much money is owed by each customer, and how long the unpaid invoices have been languishing. The length of time that money remains unpaid is called *aging*. Often referred to as "money on the street", a large balance in your A/R report can have a serious effect on your ability to continue operations.

The best use of this report is to develop a plan to contact the customers with the oldest and/or largest balances and make an effort to collect the money owed to you. You should also think about setting credit limits for customers who traditionally hold your money for a long time; once the credit limit is reached, orders must be paid for in advance or sent COD.

Too many business owners are reluctant to "cut off" customers who have owed a lot of money for a long time by insisting on advance payments or just refusing to continue to provide products or services until the customer has caught up. These owners are afraid that if they cut off a customer they lose all chance of recovering the money currently owed. Many of these owners end up mired in customer debt, because these customers really aren't going to catch up whether you continue to provide goods and services or not. Once it's obvious that a customer doesn't pay your invoices, stop selling to them (except for cash sales).

Proving the A/R Report Total Against the Balance Sheet

When you create an A/R report, make sure you also create a balance sheet report with the same date for both reports. The total aging in the A/R report must match the A/R amount on the balance sheet. If the amounts don't match, you must find out why. Following are some useful methods to track down the problem.

Change the date range of both reports, going back to the last day of the month previous to the date you originally selected for the reports.

- If the account totals match, you know that your problem is in the month ending on the original date for the reports.

- If the account totals don't match, go back another month (or several months) until you find a month end date where the totals match. Your problem is in transactions later than that date.

- If you can't find any month in the recent past where the totals match, call your accountant for advice.

In the "problem month(s)", look for journal entries that contain a posting to the A/R account. Those amounts will be part of the A/R total on the balance sheet, but shouldn't show up in the A/R aging report because the A/R aging report is a report on transactions that went to sales journals and cash receipts journals. (The aging report is built "up" from transaction journals, not "down" from amounts in the general ledger.)

If you're using accounting software, make sure you haven't changed the report settings for either the balance sheet or the A/R aging report to filter the report in any way.

If you're not using accounting software (which automatically posts invoices and invoices payments to A/R), look for a sales transaction or a payment transaction in which you accidentally selected an account other than A/R.

Accounts Payable Report

The Accounts Payable (A/P) report displays all the vendor bills you've entered into your system that you haven't yet paid. The report also displays the length of time that each bill has remained unpaid.

Use this report to determine which bills should be paid if you don't have enough cash on hand to pay all your bills. The decision is based as much on your relationship with, or need for, vendors as on the amount of the balance due.

As with A/R, the total amount of A/P must equal the A/P amount displayed on the balance sheet for the same date. If the totals don't match, use the suggestions in the previous section on A/R to troubleshoot the problem.

Inventory Reports

If you track inventory, you need to keep an eye on inventory data. The most important report is the inventory valuation report, which displays the asset value of the current quantity on hand for each item (see Figure 11-4). The total asset value in this report must match the value of the Inventory Asset account on your balance sheet for the same date.

If the values don't match you need to search transactions involving inventory to see where the problem occurred. Look for a journal entry with a posting entry to the inventory asset account (the most common cause of this problem).

There is no situation in which the value of your inventory asset should be changed via a J/E, because a J/E doesn't adjust quantity. If you find a J/E, ask the person who created it about the purpose of the adjustment (of course, that person may be you). Void the J/E and enter a transaction that's appropriate to the purpose of the J/E to adjust the inventory. (Chapter 8 explains how to adjust inventory.)

An "appropriate" transaction is one in which both quantity and value are adjusted, and the most common adjustments are the following:

- An inventory adjustment transaction after a physical count.

- An inventory adjustment transaction when you remove inventory for your own use.

- A customer credit for the return of inventory.

- A customer credit for damaged inventory that isn't returned by the customer.

Inventory Valuation Summary

	On Hand	Avg Cost	Asset Value
Inventory			
Gadget01	1	100.00	100.00
Gadget02	8	67.60	540.80
Monitor	3	54.00	162.00
NIC			
3COM NIC	5	30.00	150.00
NE2000 NIC	0	28.00	0.00
NIC - Other	0	0.00	0.00
Total NIC	5		150.00
Sound Card	6	40.00	240.00
KVM	5	250.00	1,250.00
VideoCard	0	60.00	0.00
Widgets	64	1.00	64.00
Total Inventory	92		2,506.80
Assembly			
kit1	0	0.00	0.00
Kit5	1	150.80	150.80
Total Assembly	1		150.80
TOTAL	**93**		**2,657.60**

Figure 11-4: The inventory asset value must match the inventory asset amount on your balance sheet.

Other important inventory reports you should view periodically are those that display the current quantity on hand and the prices of inventory items. Here are some guidelines that most business owners find helpful:

- Periodically run reports that show the profit per item, and adjust the pricing of items that are showing less profit because of rising costs.

- If seasonal products lack enough quantity on hand to fill the rush of orders you expect, make sure you order more in a timely fashion. Your suppliers are probably facing large shipments of the same seasonal items to your competitors.

- For non-seasonal products, make sure you've set realistic reorder points (the level of quantity on hand at which you reorder) so you don't ever lose a sale because you're out of stock.

- Keep an eye on backorders to make sure enough product is due in to fill them and restock for future orders.

TIP: Make sure you track the backorders that are filled to make sure that some customers aren't being neglected when new products arrive in insufficient quantity to fill all backorders. Some sales reps tend to manipulate the way backorders are filled in favor of their own customers.

Bank Reconciliation

Business owners should always go over the bank statement and the bank register and compare them. Unlike the other reports discussed in this chapter, you don't view the bank statement to check figures and analyze them. Instead, this is a security check.

Unfortunately, statistics show that the rate of embezzlement in small businesses is much higher than you'd guess (and higher than embezzlement rates in large businesses). Even worse, a large percentage of embezzlers are family members who work in the family business.

According to a report from the Association of Certified Fraud Examiners, businesses lose 7% of their annual revenues to fraud, and small businesses are especially vulnerable. The median loss suffered by small businesses was estimated at $200,000 per business, which is higher, on average, than the amounts large companies lose.

According to the U.S. Chamber of Commerce, check tampering and fraudulent billing (the most common small business fraud schemes) destroy many small businesses. The American Management Association estimates that one-third of small business bankruptcies and at least twenty percent of business failures are due to employee theft.

Examining the Bank Statement

The bank statement contains check numbers (without names) for checks you sent to vendors, and payee names for electronic transfers. Pictures of the checks (both front and back) are usually included in the statement or can be ordered from the bank.

Look for vendor names that appear frequently. Look for vendor names that only appear occasionally where the amounts seem to be unusually large. Look for vendor names that aren't familiar to you. Check those vendor records in your accounting system. What's the address and telephone number and what do you buy from them? Call the vendor if the name isn't familiar to you.

Look for bank transfers between bank accounts and make sure all the banks listed for these transfers are your own bank accounts.

Compare checks on the statement to the bank register and be suspicious of a check that was entered into the register months earlier than the check cleared; this indicates a back-dated check. A back dated check is designed to be hard to spot, because the last time you checked the bank register it didn't exist. This is especially suspicious if the check date in your system is for the previous year and the check was cashed this year (business owners hardly ever create reports for the previous year so they don't see back-dated transactions).

TIP: If you use accounting software, after you reconcile the statement the software prints a bank reconciliation report that lists the items in your bank register that have not yet cleared the bank. You can check this list for older items instead of going through the bank register.

Imposing Bank Account Security Measures

Large companies lose less to fraud than small companies because they have sufficient personnel to impose policies that make fraud more difficult. For example, the person with software permissions to add a new vendor to the accounting system does not have permission to write checks or approve vendor bills. The person with permission to approve vendor bills and enter them into the system does not have permission to write checks.

The budget and personnel constraints on a small business make security measures of this type difficult. There are, however, some security measures you can impose as the business owner.

Don't set up your bank accounts for electronic statements unless you can configure that feature for a different password than the password used for creating electronic transactions and viewing/downloading reports. Don't give anyone else the password. Unfortunately, most banks don't offer password security measures for different types of features, and if your bank doesn't offer this security measure, insist on paper statements.

If you receive paper statements, have the bank statement sent to your residence instead of the office. In fact, it's best if you reconcile the account every month. If that's not possible, when you bring the statement to the person who reconciles the bank (probably the same person who writes the checks), stay in the room while the reconciliation proceeds. Ask questions about any transaction you're suspicious about. In fact, ask questions about most of the transactions, just to create the ambiance "I'm watching carefully", because that reduces the level of temptation.

If your accountant is reconciling your bank accounts for you, the process is probably just a mathematical procedure to him or her. Accountants cross-reference the transactions on the bank statement to matching amounts in your ledgers. Your own familiarity with vendors and customers makes it easier for you to spot potential security problems. Make sure you have a copy of the statement so you can scan it for names or transactions you don't recognize or seem out of the ordinary.

Look in the bank register for missing check numbers. Then call the bank or check old statements to see if the check was presented. Look in the bank register for checks marked VOID and call the bank or check old statements to see if the check was presented. Keep a list of missing check numbers and voided checks and check future statements for these transactions.

Look at the checks you purchased and make sure the number of the last check matches the order you placed. It's not uncommon for people to help themselves to checks from the bottom of the pack for nefarious reasons.

Peachtree and QuickBooks, the two most popular software programs for small businesses, permit users to delete transactions (including checks). Most high-end accounting software permits users to void checks, but not to delete them (a check marked VOID, with a zero amount, is easy to spot when you look at the bank register, but a deleted check is just "not there").

However, both Peachtree and QuickBooks have a feature called "audit trail report" that produces a report for every transaction created, changed, voided, or deleted. Make it a habit to look at this report at least once a week.

Audit trails don't work unless users sign in to the accounting software with unique names (the audit trail includes the name of the user who created each transaction). In addition to forcing unique names, impose (and enforce) a rule that no user can leave his or her desk without closing the software. This prevents anyone else from accessing the software and creating transactions (or deleting transactions) under another user's name.

Not all "date lags" indicate a security issue. Sometimes there's a non-threatening reason that a transaction is still uncleared after a long period of time. Are you storing a customer's check in your desk instead of depositing it (either inadvertently or for some reason) while your software shows it was deposited more than a month ago? Is a vendor insisting the payment you sent months ago was not received, even though your books show that you paid the bill and don't have an outstanding balance? It's possible the postal service failed (or maybe the check is stored in the vendor's desk).

Index

Index

Index

disposition of fixed assets, 205–208, 225

distributions from equity, 144, 147–148, 149–150. See also withdrawals (draws) from
      equity

dividend payments to stockholders, 147–148

divisionalized chart of accounts, 21–25, 39

DM (debit memo), 79

double-entry bookkeeping, defined, 1

draw on equity. See withdrawals (draws) from equity

draw on line of credit, 126–127

E

electronic funds transfer (EFT), 64

electronic payments to vendors, 64–68

embezzlement, detecting, 238

employee vs. independent contractor status, 184–187

employees. See payroll

E-Pay payments, 65

equity
      balancing with liabilities, 226–229
      corporations, 145–150
      LLCs and LLPs, 138–144
      overview, 6–7, 129–131
      partnerships, 135–138
      proprietorships, 131–135
      year-end allocations, 212–213

escrow fund tracking, 113–116

Excel, Microsoft, 27

expenses. See also disbursements; payments
      and accounting method choice, 11–12
      bad debt expense, 90–91
      credits from vendors, 69–70, 96, 176
      debit cards, 78–81
      defined, 55
      directors' fees as, 147
      interest on loans, 125
      interest paid on line of credit, 127
      overhead allocation at year's end, 211–212
      overview, 8–10, 55–56
      payroll posting, 189, 193–196
      personal expenses paid from equity, 133–135, 138
      petty cash, 71–78
      P&L report analysis, 231–232
      prepaid, 4–5, 96–97
      reimbursing independent contractors for, 200–201
      sold inventory items as, 158

Index

Index

expense categories for deduction, 8–9
forms needed, 214–220
guaranteed payment reporting, 143–144
and independent contractors, 15, 186–187, 197–200, 215
paying out of proprietorship, 134
profit or loss as basis for, 130
S corporations, 150, 219–220
sales, 33–36
trust fund, 190–192
use tax tracking, 118–123
terms of payment for customers, 33
threshold amount for Form 1099 reporting, 197
TIN (tax identification number), 199
trademarks, patents, and copyrights, 102–103
transactions. See also sales transactions
amortization, 203–205
depreciation, 203–205
divisionalized chart of account postings, 24–25
entering basics, 1–3
journal entries from, 27–28
overview, 25–26
split, 60–61
transfer, 84–85
transferring money between accounts, 83–85
trial balance, defined, 29–30
trust fund taxes, 190–192
trust (escrow) fund tracking, 113–116
type of customer designation, 38

U
upfront deposits
from customers, 108–110
to vendors, 94–95
use tax tracking, 118–123

V
valuation of inventory, 160–166, 235–236
value of inventory, tracking, 156–157
variable expenses, 231–232
vendor codes, 56–57
vendors
creating, 56–58
deposits made to, 94–95
naming, 56–58
optional information, 59